Inspirational Stories from the Heart of Aloha

BEING LOCAL IN HAWAI`I

"Talking Story" with Julia of Wahiawa

Keiko Matsui Higa

Inspirational Stories from the Heart of Aloha: Being Local in Hawai'i Talking "Story" with Keiko Matsui Higa
© 2014

Disclaimer: All websites referenced in this book are not maintained or owned by the author and may have changed since the publication of this book.

Cover Layout & Interior Design: Fusion Creative Works, fusioncw.com
Cover Design: Nicole Gabriel
Photographer: Robert Matsui Estrella (Baha'i gardens and shrines and recent family photos)

ISBN: 978-1-940984-15-5

Published by
AVIVA Publishing
Lake Placid, New York.
www.avivapubs.com

Printed in the United States of America

This book is dedicated to:

Palikapu Dedman, Oscar López Rivera,
Yuri Kochiyama, and Kekuni Blaisdell

Acknowledgments

A big "mahalo" to my son, Robert, who has been my biggest supporter for the last forty-five years. Words cannot express the gratitude I have for his never failing assistance in whatever project I undertook and continue to undertake.

Thank you to my husband, Roger, who unfortunately died of a stroke in the year 2002. Roger and Robert were inseparable and they kept our family in balance and harmony. The word "interdependence" has been my mantra all these years because of these two wonderful souls in my life.

This book would not have been published in a timely manner had I not attended the Baha'i School this past summer in Eliot, Maine. For all the support and ideas I received from the participants in the "Spirit of Children" class, I am most grateful, especially for Phyllis Ring, who emerged as one of my editors.

I thank Nia Aitaoto for her networking skills in setting up speaking engagements for me and in her overall support in writing this book.

Thanks also to Patrick Snow and his organization for guiding me to finish this book in five months, an incredible feat. Mahalo to Patrick and the rest of the Snow team: Tyler Tichelaar, who did the final edit; Nicole Gabriel for her front cover design that truly captured the book's essence; Shiloh Schroeder, who created the beautiful interior layout; and Susan Friedmann of Aviva Publishing for being my publisher.

And finally, "Thank you" to all our family's friends and relatives—our extended ʻohana—who made our life experiences so meaningful and rich.

Robert "Bob" Estrella and Mochi—Our favorite dog.

CONTENTS

PART THREE: THE FLOWERING TREE: SERVICE

PART FOUR: HEALTH IS EVERYTHING

APPENDICES

Prologue

KŪKANILOKO... "TO ANCHOR THE CRY FROM WITHIN"

by
Jo-Lin Lenchanko Kalimapau
Historian, Hawaiian Civic Club of Wahiawa

Līhu'e, Wahiawā, Halemano—sacred uplands—the birthplace of the highest ruling chiefs distinguished by the *ka`ananiau*: a beautiful place in time. Kūkaniloko is one of the most sacred sites in all of the Hawai'i Islands. This site, *kapaahuawa,* was first associated with the birth of Kapawa to *Ali`i* Nanakaoko and his wife, *Ali`i* Kahikiokalani in A.D.1060. For more than 500 years, here in these sacred uplands, the purity of royal lineages was maintained, giving chiefs their godly status and the right to be leaders. The child born in the presence of these chiefs was called an *ali`i,* an *akua,* a *wela*—a chief, a god, a blaze of heat. (Kamakau 1991:38) Cultivation of pineapple in the mid-1900s resulted in the destruction of the temple, *waihau heiau Ho`olonopahu.* Here at this temple, the recitation of genealogies since time immemorial, time eternal took place; here the *piko,* umbilical cord, was ceremonially cut; and here the sacred temple drums of Hāwea and 'Ōpuku announced the birth of the royal child.

Kūkaniloko encompasses 36,000 acres. Boundaries are defined in our chants and *mo`olelo*—traditional comprehension. The five acre parcel now known as Kūkaniloko Birthstones State Monument is located to the North of Wahiawā Town. Preservation and enhancement measures, implemented by the Hawaiian Civic Club of Wahiawā for more than four generations, protect and preserve this sacred site in perpetuity. As knowledgeable representatives sensitive to traditional site and land management, we choose to act responsibly without compromising the respect and sensitivity of our Nation, *ko Hawai`i paeaina.* We look to the voice of our *kupuna ma*—those whom we choose to follow—who left us with this reflection:

Respect is unconditional love handed down from generation to generation...

Kūkaniloko, the *piko,* metaphysically centered and connected since time immemorial, time eternal, emanates *Aloha,* the greatest truth of all...*eō it only begins...*

"e kuka'awe i nā kapu o Kūkaniloko no ka mea aloha no ho'i kākou ia lākou i nā kau a kau..." "to guard the kapu of Kūkaniloko because we love them for all time...."

Introduction

Growing up in Wahiawa, my favorite spot was the Wahiawa Library and the gulch behind it. I am amazed that my sister and I were able to run down the gulch to the other side barefoot, especially with thick tree trunks protruding all over the place.

During the summer months, I was checking out books on an almost daily basis (except for Sundays). At one point, I felt I had read almost every book in the children's section.

My uniqueness in enjoying books lay in the fact that I was a "smeller" of books. I loved the smell of books, especially the ones hot off the press. Thus, my addiction early on was the smell of *The Jennifer Wish*. For over fifty years, I would search for this title in every library I visited. I finally found it listed at the Library of Congress, but unfortunately, I could not purchase the book or borrow it. More recently, I was able to go online and actually purchase a copy at a very high price. I eagerly turned to open the book upon arrival—the smell was not there! Nevertheless, the wonderful illustrations and stories were there and the wonderful memory of childhood flooded back. It was worth the high price.

If only all of childhood could be as wonderful as the smell of that book! But I had some unpleasant experiences as well. Hawai'i has always been a diverse and multicultural environment, and I have lived my life in the midst of cultural diversity...and sadly, some cultural conflicts. The photo of the sea turtle on this book's cover, taken by my son Bob, is very special to me because it represents the bi-cultural nature of my life. Just as the sea turtle can navigate the ocean and enjoy being on land as well as the ocean, I have learned how to navigate Asian and Western culture. It has been an amazing learning experience and one I hope you will agree is well worth sharing.

This book is the result of my desire to share how I have navigated these two cultures, learning from both and understanding what it is to belong to each one. In these pages, I will share with my readers my experience growing up as a Japanese-American in Hawai'i with an Okinawan mother and later a Filipino husband. I have known what it is to experience racism, and I have known what it is to experience the many joys of life. Most importantly, I believe that our lives have a purpose and any adversities we face will only make us stronger. The wisdom gathered from those adversities needs to be passed on to help others learn and heal their lives. That important need to tell our stories is why I refer to "talking story" in my subtitle.

They say that everyone wants to write a book, but few people do. For many years, I thought it would be too daunting a task to write a professional-looking book and find a publisher.

You might feel the same way. So I gave up on the idea until I attended the Spirit of Children retreat and met so many creative people, many of whom were published authors and artists. Then I met Patrick Snow at Manoa Library in Honolulu, where he presented twenty-one mistakes that most of us make in writing and publishing a book. Then he presented solutions to each of those mistakes, and I had a "Yes" moment. I said, "Yes" to all my dreams of wanting to be a writer, knowing that it was not as impossible as my mind had made me believe.

I was also inspired by the Bamboo Ridge collective and press, based in Hawai'i, which publishes journals twice a year with contributions from many local artists and writers. Bamboo Ridge is a nonprofit, tax-exempt corporation formed in 1978 to foster the appreciation, understanding, and creation of literary, visual, or performing arts by, for, or about Hawai'i's people. One can subscribe to the journal by writing to: brinfo@bambooridge.com or www.bambooridge.com.

Also, in keeping with my obsession over the smell of books, I have decided to bless each of my books "hot off the press" with several drops of Wild Orange or Peppermint essential oils. (I'll share more about my love for essential oils in this book.) There are 250 drops in each doTerra bottle so it will only cost around ten cents for each blessing. And since these are Certified Therapeutic Pure Grade (CTPG) drops, there will be no problems with drug-sniffing dogs at the airport. I hope I am starting a "movement" of sorts in appreciating the power of the smell of "pure" nature (no perfumes, please).

Most importantly, I hope that my writing this book will encourage readers to tell their own stories. I believe it's true that everyone has a book inside him or her. But even if you don't publish a book yourself, it is important that you write down your story to pass on to others and so future generations can learn from it. That's what "talking story" is all about—telling our stories so we can share our wisdom and make the world a better place. The world will be richer when common ordinary people like you and me can share our life experiences and then learn from and build on them.

In this day of Facebook, Twitter, and blogs, I am hoping that some of my readers will want to interact with me by sending me questions, comments, recommendations for the next edition, and sharing snippets of their stories as well.

I look forward to the interaction with my readers and hope to learn a lot from such sharing. Come "talk story" with me by visiting and commenting at: www.keikomatsuihiga.com and www.thatdoterragal.com

Mahalo to all my relatives....for when you participate in reading this book, you join 'ohana (extended family) circle.

Julia Keiko Matsui Higa Estrella

March 3, 2014

Part One

DEEP ROOTS

"As long as we have life,
We must do our utmost
To combat the schemes
Of the dark forces
Which are trying
To destroy the world."

— Mokichi Okada

My Mother: Matsuo Higa Matsui

Wedding Photo: Kyozo and Matsuo Matsui

Growing up in Okinawa, my mother had some exciting stories to tell. She was born in 1900 in Kita-Nakagusuku, in the center of the main island of Okinawa, ruled by Japan. She left Okinawa around 1917 to marry an Okinawan man from the same village who was working as an early immigrant in the sugar plantation of Waipahu, Hawai'i. "Picture Bride" was a title given to many of the women who arrived, like my mother, as the result of an exchange of photos between a prospective bride and groom.

Matsuo is a name given only to men, so I asked my mother how she ended up with "Matsuo" on her green card. She explained that there were two girls at the elementary school with the name Matsu and the teacher just decided to call one of them Matsu and my mother became Matsuo. Her elementary school was located on the grounds of the famous Nakagusuku Castle, a place tourists now visit to experience some of the early history of Okinawa.

Her family name was "Higa," but the indigenous pronunciation is "Fija," and it means "laughter and happiness." Her family claimed to be descended from the famous Samurai clan named "Tametomo no Minamoto." It seemed incredulous to me that one could come from such nobility. Nonetheless, the family would proudly show its clan burial site at a certain cave, which was known to be the Tametomo burial site. Even if my mother were indeed from this Tametomo line, the fact of the matter was that her family was very poor, living in a mud hut and often surviving at the point of starvation. My grandmother would go to a funeral and hide food in her kimono to bring home to feed her children. Thus, without much food to go around, it was natural for her family to urge my mother to become a picture bride, with the hopes that she would be able to send money home from a job in Hawai'i.

My mother had one daughter and two sons from this first picture bride marriage to Mr. Asato. Husband and wife both tried to earn enough money to send back to impoverished homes in Okinawa. As children arrived, they would be sent to

Okinawa at an early age to be raised by Grandmother. There was no child care system on the plantations, so in order to continue working in the fields, most mothers had to send children back to the homeland to be nurtured by relatives.

My mother was so resourceful that she was able to save enough money to send small amounts to her family with the instruction to buy land. Her salary as a "weeder" was fifty cents for a ten-hour day, while her husband as a cane hauler made seventy-five cents a day.

One day while Matsuo was weeding the rows of sugarcane, she heard her babies crying from a distance. Women in those days brought their babies with them to work and left them on blankets under a tree.

When she rushed over to see why the babies were crying, Matsuo spotted a mongoose near the blanket looking at the bawling babies. She ended up laughing at what she saw. Chasing the mongoose away, she picked up the two babies and comforted them. Then she went back to work.

After seventeen years on the plantation, my mother and Mr. Asato returned to Okinawa. They owned land now, but this fact caused a big rift in their marriage. According to Okinawan custom, a man could have mistresses if he owned land. Having converted to Christianity in Hawai'i, my mother would not tolerate the presence of young mistresses in the household, especially since much of the land had been earned from her hard work and her ability to save money. The final blow arrived when her younger son died of internal injuries at a judo practice; my mother pled for her son to be taken to the hospital, but her husband refused.

This death was the last straw for my mother. She wrote to a Reverend Shimatori in Wahiawa, asking whether he could sponsor her so she could return to Hawai'i. Fortunately, he said, "Yes" and a new life lay ahead of her.

However, as punishment, Mr. Asato forbade my mother to bring her daughter, Mineko, and her son, Hiroshi, to Hawai'i with her. She was heartbroken, but she had no recourse. I cried when my mother described to me the scene at the port in Okinawa on departure day. No one was allowed to come to say "goodbye," so Matsuo stood forlornly by herself as she waited to board the ship. Only the Christian pastor arrived in time to bid her goodbye and wish her a safe journey to Hawai'i. She arrived at the port of Honolulu on December 10, 1936 to start a new life.

The good news is that Rev. Shimatori introduced my mother to Kyozo Matsui from the Hiroshima prefecture in Japan, and then the reverend acted as their "go-between." From Hawai'i, my mother divorced Mr. Asato, a brave thing to do in those days when wives were not allowed to divorce their husbands.

My mother married my father, Kyozo, in 1937. Thus, my father and my mother were both approaching forty when they started a new family. My sister arrived on April 20, 1939, and I joined the family on December 26, 1940. Rev. Shimatori chose for us the names Ruth Hatsue from the Old Testament and Julia Keiko from the New Testament. However, my family and the local Japanese-Okinawan community knew me by my Japanese name, Keiko. Then when I began school and entered the Euro-American world, I became known to my classmates as Julia Matsui.

While I was growing up, Rev. Hirano and his son, David, would come to our home in Wahiawa on a regular basis, representing the Holiness Church. Apparently Rev. Hirano was sent as a missionary from Japan to Hawai'i. My mom told me that Rev. Hirano was the one who converted her to Christianity. What a small world because twenty-five years later, Rev. Hirano's son, David, and I would be working closely together on the national level of the Pacific Islander and Asian American Ministries (PAAM) of the United Church of Christ. Both of us started out as children active in the Holiness church, lost track of each other, and ended up working on various councils of the Congregational system many years later. David also experienced a lot of institutional racism while serving as head of Global Ministries but we will leave it to David to tell his own story one of these days in his own book.

Fortunately for my sister and me, there were no boys born into the family since boys were given preferential treatment in Japanese culture in those days. Instead, we were both treated with much love because it was the first family for my father and the second family for my mother.

And because our parents were no longer young, I think Ruth and I were treated almost like grandchildren. It was a blessing indeed to have mellow parents who came with a lot of life experience and wisdom.

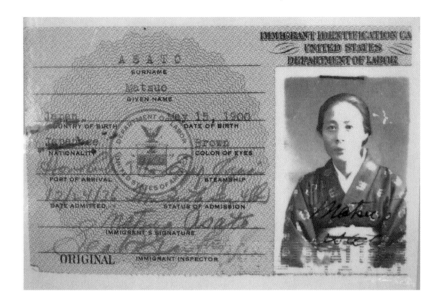

Higa family in Kitanakagusuku, Okinawa.
Julia in purple, on a visit to Okinawa in 2011.

Higa family in Tokyo; left to right, Akiko, Junji, Derrick, Alyssa.

My Father: Kyozo Matsui

KYOZO MATSUI

Leaving his village of Kobatake in Japan at the tender age of thirteen must have been very difficult for my father, Kyozo Matsui. Being the youngest son, however, Kyozo knew that he would not inherit any of the family land. Thus the words on the posters recruiting young men to work in the fields of Hawai'i pointed to a good deal and the promise of a lucrative job. Little did he know how hard the work would be as a cane hauler in the hot sun of Hawai'i. So young Kyozo set off down the mountain path and walked many miles before he reached the port near Hiroshima.

Once he left, Kyozo never looked back. When he died at the age of eighty-eight, he was totally out of touch with his relatives in Kobatake. And because he never shared any stories with Ruth and me, we knew practically nothing about his childhood. We did not have any address or letters from his family or friends—we didn't even know the name of his village until recently.

Finding my relatives from my father's side turned into a miracle story. I was not interested in finding my relatives in Hiroshima until a friend said it was important to know your roots and be part of your ancestors on both sides of the family.

I reflected on the "roots" issue and put it on the back burner since I did not know how to take the first step. I realized searching for my father's family was a seemingly "impossible" task since I could not read much Japanese.

Then the miracle began. I met a Korean woman, born and raised in Japan, who was working on her degree in cultural studies and women's studies. Yeonghae Jung enrolled for two years at UC-Berkeley to further her studies. And because she needed a place to stay, we offered a room to her and her three-year-old daughter.

We became a tight-knit family, and when Yeonghae returned to Japan, I asked her to do a little research and find out the name of my father's village. All she had to work with was my father's name. She wrote back and said that my father came from a mountain village called Kobatake in the Hiroshima prefecture. I was elated at this discovery and asked whether there was any possibility she could meet me at a train station in the Aichi area. The second question was whether she would be able to drive me up the mountain trail to Kobatake.

Yeonghae turned out to be my angel. Miles and miles of upward-curving roadway was a difficult drive, but after two or more hours, we reached Kobatake.

Upon arrival, Yeonghae and I were amazed at the sheer beauty of the place—clean running streams, beautiful flowers, and trees everywhere. I wondered why my father would ever want to leave such a beautiful place. It seemed even more lovely than Hawai'i. Indeed, it was my image of the Garden of Eden.

After refreshing ourselves, Yeonghae and I set out to find people who might have known my father as a youth. I had only one photo of my father, on his wedding day, plus a faded family tree called the "koseki." My friends, who later heard how I engaged in the search, said I had so much "chutzpah" since I went from shop to shop, showing the shopkeepers my father's photo and asking whether anyone in the area resembled him.

After several hours of no results, Yeonghae pointed to the late-afternoon sky and indicated that it would be difficult for her to drive back down the curving road at night. I begged to visit one more store and she said, "Yes, but make it short." Amazingly, this last shopkeeper pointed down the road and said that there was a "look alike" in a nearby senior home.

Desperate for a positive outcome, I prayed that the gentleman would indeed turn out to be a relative. When I showed the photo to the receptionist at the senior home, she immediately called a room number, and in a few minutes, in walked a gentleman with exactly the same smile as Kyozo.

I told the receptionist, "This is my long lost relative!" Then we looked at the family tree and found the name "Tadami" on the chart. On this "koseki," Tadami was listed as my father's brother's grandson.

Meanwhile, it was turning dark outside, so I apologized profusely to my newly-found relative, Tadami, indicating the need to get home safely to Hiroshima city.

However, Tadami insisted that he be allowed to take us to my father's childhood home, although it was rundown and vacant. Yeonghae nodded, "Okay." Tadami had just retired from being a taxicab driver and like a true Japanese taxi driver, he whipped himself quickly around the mountain while Yeonghae followed suit.

As we approached the birthplace of Kyozo, we saw three men standing outside the gate as though they were expecting us. Amazingly, the three men had arrived to pay their respects to their ancestors on that day and were planning to go to the cemetery to clean the family plots and place flowers there.

We introduced ourselves and discovered we were cousins. Then we quickly exchanged addresses and apologized that we needed to get down the mountain before darkness descended. We hurriedly took a photo of the three men with the abandoned home in the background.

Little did we know that thirteen years later, Ayako, the daughter of one of the men, would be living with us in Kapolei, Hawai'i, while studying English at the Leeward Community College. When Ayako's sister, Tomoko, visited us in February 2013, she took many photos of the three of us visiting my hometown of Wahiawa. One of the men was Tokumi Matsui, Tadami's son. Recently, Tokumi and his wife Junko spent a week with us over the Christmas holidays (Christmas 2013) in Kapolei, Hawaii. It was such a memorable experience; I marvel at how fortunate Bob and I are to be able to connect with Tokumi, Junko, Ayako, and Tomoko, long lost relatives.

Tomoko is a budding artist and I have included her art work in color. Please visit her blog at katazomeir.exblog.jp and help her to be more than a "budding" artist. She paints scenes of her father, her mother, and her neighborhood in a very whimsical style. She also did a postcard with the Tokyo Sky Tree on it because her father was one of the many engineers who made Tokyo Sky Tree possible. His story was in one of the publications from Japan, but because I cannot read the "kanji" in the book, I was not able to get the details of his contribution. Please google "Tokyo Sky Tree" and you will find many interesting stories about how it is the tallest building in Japan and possibly the second tallest building in the world. The family's photo has been attached to this story.

This experience is part of why I have become a believer in miracles—in the power and purpose, in the unexpected twists and turns that have led ultimately to inexplicable outcomes in my life.

Wilfred and Amy Kusaka, children of Sensei Kusaka and Mineko Asato

Tokumi and Junko Matsui and their children Ayako and Tomoko,
during a visit to Hawai'i Christmas 2013.

Visit Tomoko's blog at www.keikomatsuihiga.com

Sisters: Peas in a Pod

Born a year and a half after my sister Ruth, I always felt some-what guilty for taking my mother's milk away from her. I was breastfed from that day until I was four, according to my mother. She had to put hot pepper on her breasts in order to force my weaning process since kindergarten was around the corner.

I think if longitudinal medical studies had been done on my sister and me as to the benefits of breast milk compared to cow's milk, we would be in line with the majority of the studies that indicate that breast milk strengthens the immune system for both the short and long term. While my sister missed many days of school because of asthma and colds, I probably missed a total of one day per school year, except for a bout with measles and mumps. This pattern of wellness due to mother's milk has carried on into almost seven decades of living.

Although I was shorter than my older sister, many people on the streets would greet us as though we were twins. My mother was a good seamstress and we had no money to buy clothes. So because my mother sewed the same outfits for both of us, we were often dressed as though we were twins.

Our favorite outfit was the pinafore—the rage in the early 1940s. No wonder my favorite book in those early years was *The Jennifer Wish* by Eunice Young Smith. The novel is illustrated with Jennifer's sister—Holly—wearing pinafores. Our least favorite outfits were skirts sewn from rice bags. In the 1950s, rice bags came with flower designs on them, so my practical mother insisted they made lovely skirts. However, no one else wore rice bags to school, so my sister and I were often embarrassed by this sign of poverty. The rice-bag skirts became more common for us to wear when we entered junior high school, a period when we were sensitive to the need to be "popular" and the effects of peer pressure in school.

Ruth and I often envied other children whose parents could speak English. We stood out from the crowd because we were one of the few children who had "Issei" (first generation) parents, making us "Nisei" (second generation). By the late 1940s, most of our classmates were "Sansei" (third generation). There was a big cultural divide in the thinking of first-generation parents and second-generation parents. Needless to say, Ruth and I felt "different" in this milieu of the Sansei generation, who seemed more modern and "hip."

The sense of not fitting in with the Sansei crowd led to our extreme shyness. My sister was voted "the most shy" every May in high school when the special edition of the *Leilehua Sentinel* came out. Fortunately, I was spared the title because my claim to fame was my studiousness.

My sister and I were often seen as "two peas in a pod" because we did everything together. We were indeed inseparable for the first eighteen years. I had even drawn a picture in my mind that when we became adults and got married, we would live right next door to each other with a wooden bridge connecting our two homes. And every day we would be busy visiting each other and acting like two peas in a pod, with our children in tow.

Such a fairyland was never to be. When my sister decided to get married the year after she graduated from high school and move to Gardena, California, I felt totally betrayed. She had never dated while in high school so her classmates were shocked to hear that the "shyest girl in the class of 1957" was the first one to get married. While I was also taken aback by this new development, I knew I was the one who had talked my dad into allowing Ruth to start dating during her first year at Hawai'i Business College.

As Issei, my parents did not believe in the concept of "dating." To this day, I don't know how I convinced my father. All I remember is that Ruth began dating a fellow student at the college who was ten years her senior, and I was the main instigator.

Little did I know that husband to be—Douglas Murakami—
would take my sister far, far away to southern California.

The closeness between my sister and me was reenacted when I
stopped by in southern California on my way to a Methodist
deputation project a few years later. Ruth came to the Los
Angeles airport to greet our deputation team. When we saw
each other, we looked at each other and cried and cried—
tears of great happiness. Onlookers must have wondered at
our streams of tears and why we did not hug each other. (We
don't hug in Japanese culture; we bow and cry if we are extremely happy.) Only those who are Issei and Nisei could have
interpreted the scene correctly as a happy reunion between
two sisters who had been inseparable for eighteen years.

Peas in a pod, we had now been thrown out of that pod into
a much larger universe.

175 Kuahiwi Street, Wahiawa, home where Julia and Ruth were born and raised. The home was sold to neighbors around 1975 and is still standing.

Matsuo and Kyozo's great grandchildren,
who live in the Los Angeles area.

World War II Hits Home

I was delivered by a midwife, Mrs. Tanji, on Dec. 26, 1940 at our home, 175 Kuahiwi Avenue in Wahiawa, located in the very center of the island of Oahu. Schofield Army Base and Hickam Air Force Base were both located in Wahiawa's backyard, so to speak, so I grew up with military families as neighbors. Since I was about to turn a year old at the time of the Pearl Harbor attack, I cannot personally remember that day, but my mother has filled in the blanks for me.

On December 7, 1941, my mother, Matsuo, was in the garden taking care of her flowerbeds when she looked up and saw many planes, and things dropping out of those planes. She did not know that these were bombs shelling military targets at both Hickam Air Base and Schofield Army Base. She commented to my father that, "The American military has such realistic practice maneuvers."

Then the sirens went off and she and my father rushed to the radio to find out why they were blaring nonstop. My parents were shocked to hear that the Japanese Air Force had flown through Kolekole Pass and was carrying out a surprise attack so close to us. The instruction to all civilians was to go immediately to their bomb shelters. Our bomb shelter was just a small hole in the ground in our garden area and had room only for two adults to huddle together with two little ones on their laps. When the sirens stopped, my parents emerged out of their shelter, but apparently, the bombing was still going on. They saw a Japanese bomber, which had been hit by artillery fire, spiraling toward a neighbor's home a block away.

Without thinking, people were rushing toward the scene rather than running away from danger. As the plane was about to crash into our neighbor's home, the kamikaze pilot looked down and waved to them, realizing that these were all Japanese families. The story seemed incredulous to me as a child, but indeed, the home was destroyed, and people on Kuahiwi Street retold the story over and over again. One of our neighbors was killed as he stood on a street corner just enjoying a beautiful sunny Sunday morning: a plane swooped down and began strafing the corner of California and Olive Streets (where the present McDonald's is located). This area was the center of "downtown," which in the '40s, encompassed a mere three short blocks for Wahiawa and was a rural community with a population of about 4,000.

Once war was declared by President Franklin Roosevelt on the day of the bombing, the fact that our family lived in such close proximity to two military bases affected my growing-up years, not only during the war years, but as long as I lived at 175 Kuahiwi Avenue. Soldiers from Schofield would march up and down Kuahiwi Street and neighboring streets as part of their weekly drill.

Perhaps I was around three when I was outfitted for a gas mask, along with all our family members. I remember sirens blaring at night when all shades had to be immediately drawn down, with Father grabbing a candle as Mother held on to my sister and me while guiding us into the makeshift bomb shelter. What child would not remember those terrifying nights, which happened quite often to ensure we were prepared for another possible attack?

During the day, as the soldiers marched up and down our street, it was another matter. I remember the soldiers smiling at us as we stood on the perimeter of our yard, waiting for one of them to toss over some candy or some gum. They must have been thinking about their own kids and missing them. We children would all be barefoot because no one could afford shoes for their children in this very low-income community.

My sister Ruth remembers military men entering homes of Japanese families and burning books written in Japanese. At our home, she was especially sad to see the precious Japanese encyclopedia going up in flames because she remembered the wonderful origami paper-folding instructions included in that multi-volume set.

Some military families preferred to live off-base with their children, so two families moved into homes across the street from ours. These families regularly beat their children and one father even used a water hose as a whip. It was horrifying to see the children run screaming and crying into the streets. Much later in life, I began to wonder whether the strict military disciplining of fathers while in training had a psychological impact leading to such terrible beatings.

As children who never experienced even a small hit on the bottom, my sister and I were shocked and mesmerized to see these regular whipping scenes. I remember one morning my sister and I lay stomach-down on our bed and asked my mother to spank us so we would know how it felt to be spanked. Needless to say, Mother just laughed and refused to do it. Perhaps that is why my sister and I never laid a hand on any of our children. Now I realize that the cruel whippings we witnessed were traumatizing events, so much so that I became a strong anti-spanking/anti-whipping advocate.

When my son Bob was about five years old, I remember my husband gave the first spank to discipline him. As he lifted his hand to give the second spank, I went out of control and threatened to divorce him immediately if another spank landed on Bob's bottom. I was probably having a post-traumatic episode from my childhood days. But my son was never spanked again, and he turned out to be a self-disciplined, happy individual who can't even recall the one spank he received.

Many other incidents affected our lives while living so close to the two military bases. As an adult, I have testified at hearings throughout Oahu against the expansion of live-fire training at Makua. Many of us also called for the step-by-step closing of military bases in Hawai'i so we would never again become a target for a surprise attack. Presently, North Korea has been saying that it has missiles that can hit Hawai'i's military arsenal. Instead of feeling more secure because we have a huge military presence on Oahu, I know that we are seen as military targets, attracting dangerous strikes against both military and nearby civilian residents.

The English Standard Test

One morning, all the students graduating from the kindergarten class in Wahiawa were put to a test. One by one, the teacher called us individually into a room and showed us pictures tacked on the classroom walls. There were pictures of horses, dogs, toys, and everyday things found in a typical home.

As the teacher pointed to each picture, the student was expected to comment on it. As a five-year-old, I did not know what this one-to-one session was all about until the following day.

Before graduation day, each of the students was informed about first grade and where we were being placed. Since my sister had graduated the year before, I had heard about a special track for students called the "English standard track." In the Wahiawa public school system, there were three tracks—the English standard track, the "A" track, and the "B" track. All the students were in the same public school system in Wahiawa Elementary, but once we were placed in a certain track, we remained in that track from first through sixth grade. The English standard track in Wahiawa ended up being filled with children from the mostly white "privileged" families, the "A" track was filled with Japanese, Korean, and Chinese students and the "B" track was made up mostly of Filipino and Hawaiian children. Institutional racism was alive and kicking in our public school system.

When I learned that I had failed the English standard test and would not be placed in that track, I was filled with anger. Somehow, I knew I was being judged unfairly—more by my race than my ability. I still marvel today that I could sense this injustice as a five-year-old. Somehow, I knew that the English standard test did not test my knowledge but was slanted against me because I was growing up in a Japanese-speaking home with a different culture from the Euro-American culture.

Part of the problem with the test is that much of it was verbal. Having been raised in a Japanese and Okinawan home, my sister and I were taught not to be too talkative. Silence was a virtue instead of constant babbling. The role of children was to "listen," not to "talk." Therefore, my answers to each picture were just one or two words—"horse," "dog," "big house," and so on. When the teacher held up a "thimble," I was stumped. I knew my mother used a thimble when she sewed; however, I did not know the English term for this sewing tool. I realized after the test that I was expected to make up a story about each picture on the wall. But it was against my culture to talk too much—brevity was the virtue emphasized in our home. Plus, I was stumped by what the English word for thimble was. To this day, I carry around a thimble to remind me of the English standard test and my first awakening to an unfair situation about which I could do very little.

However, I did not give up willingly. I asked my father, who worked as a janitor at the elementary school, to plead my case with the school principal. I knew the English standard track had better teachers, better equipment, and better excursions. I wanted an equal chance at the "best" the school could offer any student. I remember my father walking to the administration building to talk to the principal. Unfortunately, he could not speak English and, therefore, could not say much to persuade the principal.

I remember how proud I was of my father for at least attempting to speak up, in broken English, for his daughter. That vision of a janitor addressing the principal in pidgin remains forever my most precious memory of my father. I wish I could have been a fly on the wall in the principal's office that day.

As a high school student, I learned that the English standard track was started because Caucasian missionaries to Hawai'i often sent their children to San Francisco to private schools for their education. As the years went by, it was decided that it was cheaper to keep the children closer to home; however, missionary parents did not want their children to be placed in the same classrooms with children from the plantation background since pidgin was a popular form of communication.

Pidgin was as negatively perceived by the missionaries as a contagious disease.

In urban areas, an entire school would be labeled an "English standard" school. In rural areas like Wahiawa, where there was only one elementary school, tracks were created within the public school system to accommodate at least three tracks. By placing most of the Filipino and Hawaiian children in the lowest track, the public school system was participating in institutional racism. Most of the children in the lowest track "internalized" the larger society's judgment that they were somehow deficient. With much sadness, I realize now that I lost a lot as a student by not being immersed with children from all races. At least one or two Filipino and Hawaiian students were in "Track A," but most of my interaction was with Chinese, Korean, Japanese, and Okinawan children, due to the structure of the public school system in the 1940s and early '50s.

When the Nisei first came to majority power in the state legislature (around 1952), to their credit, one of the first actions taken by the new legislature was to abolish the English standard system. The Nisei understood that institutional racism undergirded such a system. I like to think that most of the Nisei legislators failed the English standard test and were also angry about the unfair education system they had experienced firsthand as children.

Failing the English standard test had one benefit for me. It made me resolve that somehow I would show the whole world that I could still outdo the Caucasian students as I entered junior high and high school, despite being "tracked" as "less than" by some unknown policymakers.

When I graduated from Leilehua High School in 1958, I looked at my father and remembered the day he walked to the principal's office to fight for his daughter's placement in the English Standard track; I was overcome with emotion and gratitude for my father's courage and love. I also recall that Mrs. Wallace Ryder Farrington, wife to the sixth territorial governor of Hawai'i, was the special speaker for our graduation. I was not aware in 1958 that she came from a long line of Euro-Americans who represented the illegal foreign occupation of the sovereign nation of Hawai'i.

My awakening to Hawai'i's political realities would only come after a long sojourn in California.

Disaster Strikes

Sensei Kusaka is in the back row, right hand side.

Why do most families have secrets? Because life is full of surprises, twists, and turns, and because thorns are always a part of one's reality.

In our family's case, what should have been a Cinderella story turned into a nightmare when World War II came to Hawai'i and all the Japanese language schools were closed because anything Japanese became suspect.

In 1940, my nineteen-year-old half-sister, Mineko, from my mother's first marriage, arrived in Hawai'i. She was so beautiful that she stole the heart of the most handsome teacher in the Wahiawa Japanese Gakuin (educational system).

All the teenage girls in the Gakuin seemed to be enthralled by Mr. Kusaka's good looks and charisma. He was indeed tall, dark, and handsome. Mineko looked like a model and Kusaka looked like a movie actor. Hearts were broken when the two decided to get married. It was truly a beautiful Cinderella story and should have had a happy ending.

Instead, tragedy struck when the Japanese language schools were banned in Hawai'i.

Kusaka could only speak Japanese and could not find a job suitable to his education. Having lost his position as a highly-respected teacher and the object of much swooning, Kusaka descended into the dark night of despair and began to drink heavily. In order to make a few bucks here and there, he went out to sea as a fisherman. Returning home, he would take out his frustration and loss of dignity on Mineko, and she became the victim of verbal and physical abuse. Fortunately, the two children—Wilfred and Amy—were not touched by their despairing and drunk father.

I clearly remember the night that Mineko arrived at our home on Kuahiwi Street with her two babies. She picked up the phone and started dialing numbers randomly as though she needed to talk to someone about her nightmare. Because she would not stop her dialing madness, my mother did not know what to do except to call for help. Mineko was taken to the Kaneohe Mental Hospital for observation. Since Japanese-speaking immigrants made up a large segment of the population of Hawai'i, it was unbelievable that the state had no Japanese-speaking psychiatrists and doctors at the hospital. All Mineko needed was crisis intervention. With no one on the medical staff able to understand or speak Japanese, electric shock therapy became the treatment of choice. In 1945, electric shock machines were a crude form of torture.

It was no surprise, therefore, that Mineko would arrive at our home on weekend passes and scream in the middle of the night as she relived the torture of being tied to a bed and being shocked over and over again.

Our family would shudder to hear her cries, and at the same time, we would feel embarrassed because the entire neighborhood probably could hear the bone-chilling screams that went on and on. Mineko became our skeleton in the closet that needed to be hid from sight.

As an adult, I would understand that the non-existence of Japanese-speaking doctors at the mental institution was another form of institutional racism.

When I took courses at the University of Hawai'i, I began to feel strongly that crisis counseling, not torture, was the treatment that would have restored Mineko to health. But because of ongoing shock treatments, she never recovered. When our family visited Mineko at the Kaneohe Institution, we saw many other young Japanese patients who seemed to have undergone shock therapy. I cry inwardly when I think of the vibrant youths and young adults who ended up like zombies for the rest of their lives, never to recover their humanity…many because they could not speak English and the staff could not speak Japanese.

Tragedy struck a second time when Kusaka was lost at sea during a heavy thunderstorm while working as a fisherman. Because his body was not found, Social Security payments were not forthcoming. Matsuo and Kyozo had to seek welfare payments because there was no food stamp program in the 1940s.

I learned from my reality as a child that no family wants to be on welfare. Therefore, it makes me sad and angry when wealthy politicians try to brainwash middle class Americans into blaming hard-working individuals—young and old—for our country's debt problem. I have hope in the near future, however, that all workers will receive a living wage. And it seems the momentum is shifting in that direction. When that happens, it will be a new day to celebrate.

Mineko Kusaaka with her children, Wilfred and Amy

Tanaka Sensei:
A Renaissance Issei Woman

When I became the student of an incredibly wise and multi-talented Issei teacher, running the ten blocks to her home at dawn became a weekly occurrence for me.

Haru Tanaka became my teacher in Japanese language and culture when I was seven. Since my parents did not speak any English except for some pidgin here and there, Japanese was the language my ears picked up from the time of birth. Nonetheless, one had to learn how to read and write Japanese, not just speak it. Therefore, Matsuo paid a small fee and enrolled my sister and me in special classes taught on Saturday mornings at the home of Tanaka Sensei. ("Sensei" is a Japanese word meaning "teacher" and used as a sign of respect.)

It soon became apparent that language was not the only thing that Sensei was passionate about. She wanted to impart to each of her students the way of the "bushido"—those who were strong, resilient, virtuous members of the Japanese community.

Sensei, therefore, encouraged her students—about thirty of us—to come as early as possible to her home. If a student showed up at 5 a.m., she would awaken and start praising the student for his or her "ganbare" (indomitable spirit). She would quickly drink some cold water, do a few "nishi shiki" (exercises), and then select a picture book from Japan that focused on one or more of the virtues esteemed by the Japanese community, such as persistence in learning a skill or compassion exhibited by a true leader.

Only three of Sensei's students, however, seemed to have the competitive urge to gain her praises. Harold Hashimoto, Charles Hirayama, and I kept showing up earlier and earlier in order to be the "first" student. Soon I was running in the dark by myself in the early dawn hours in order to get to the corner of Olive and California Avenues to reach the Top Hat Bar—Sensei's home was located right behind the Top Hat lounge. As I climbed the steps to the top of the porch, I would look for pairs of "zoris" (sandals). If there were no flip-flops at the door, then I knew I had beaten Harold or Charles.

Sensei had invented a reward system like no other I have experienced in all my years of schooling. Not only did a student get showered with praises and wonderful stories from Japan upon showing up at 6 a.m. or earlier, but Sensei would immediately start lessons after the stories were shared, even if you were the only student present.

Sensei sat at the head of a long rectangular table surrounded by stools. Because an early student received the full attention of the teacher, it meant the lessons went faster and the student could go home much earlier than students who showed up at 7 or 8 a.m. When the room was crowded with students, there would be a long line to have new words put into one's lesson book, words that would then have to be used in a variety of sentences.

The two students sitting to Sensei's right and left were allowed to thrust their lesson books in front of her at any time, and she would immediately give attention to the students as part of the reward system. Furthermore, when Sensei felt that a student had learned enough for the day, she would allow the person sitting to her right and left to give his or her stool to the person of his or her choice. This meant that the chosen person was granted the privilege of "cutting" in line, thus granting the student a powerful status. In my case, I always saved my stool for my best friends who inevitably arrived at around 8 a.m. For most students, classes would last for four or five hours unless one inherited a "privileged" stool.

During the summer, Sensei taught the girls in the class different skills such as drafting patterns and sewing one's own outfit, embroidery, crochet, flower arrangement, or doll-making. Most of us were in awe of the talented Tanaka Sensei since she knew how to do everything well. Many students were also afraid of Sensei because she could be very stern, strict, and uncompromising in setting the bar high for all her students.

During World War II, Tanaka Sensei had been interned at the Jerome Relocation Center, a concentration camp for the Japanese in Arizona. She was one of the few Japanese-Americans in Hawai'i to go to a concentration camp because she was seen as a "leader" in the islands' Japanese community. Unlike Japanese-Americans on the West Coast of the continental United States, most Japanese-Americans in Hawai'i were not interned since they served as the "cheap labor" on the sugar and pineapple plantations. I was fortunate that my parents were farm workers and not "leaders" in the community. It was not until Tanaka Sensei was released from camp in 1946 that I had the privilege of beginning classes in her home.

Even when Japanese schools reopened in the 1950s and classes were no longer held in her home, I always had the privilege of being placed in Tanaka Sensei's advanced classes at the Wahiawa Hongwanji School. These were Monday through Friday after-school classes from 3:30 to 4:30 p.m. Somehow the one-hour classes were not the same as the Saturday classes filled with stories from Japan, and with many cultural lessons.

Sensei also taught me how to use natural healing processes using the "nishi shiki" method. To this day, when I injure any part of my body, I immediately place it above my heart and start moving that part rapidly until the injured finger or foot becomes numb. More recently at the age of sixty-six, I fell down the basement stairs and injured my back. Rather than going to the doctor, I moved my back all night, long waiting for it to become numb. There is no way to move the back rapidly enough to become numb, but still, the back did heal over a two-week period without the aid of Western medicine.

Whenever I returned to Hawai'i for a visit during my long sojourn in California, I would stop by Top Hat and visit with Tanaka Sensei. My last visit was when she was around ninety-eight years old. She had just returned from a trip to Japan, and she was still walking on a regular basis to the community center near Cane Street, about a mile away. I was sorry that I was not in Hawai'i when she died at the age of 101.

Sensei's ganbare spirit still lives in me. I hope to pass it on to the generations to come.

Wilfred and Amy Kusaka and their children and grandchildren
celebrate New Year's with Julia, January 2013.

An Eye-Opening Mentor

Mentors seem to appear when called forth by one's spiritual needs. My mother and father, who surrounded Ruth and me with unconditional love all of our lives, were supplemented with other mentors as we became teenagers.

In addition to the first five years of one's life being the most important years of "formation," the other pivotal years are ages twelve to fifteen. During this time, I discovered that other adults were needed in my life as mentors, especially since these years tend to be ones when you are heavily influenced by your peers.

My sister and I were extremely shy at age twelve because our parents did not speak English, whereas most of our classmates came from English-speaking homes. We felt different because we lived in an Issei culture while most of our classmates came from a Nisei culture.

Into this mix of culture arrived Dorothy Ichinaga Thomas, a Methodist pastor's wife, who was such a different Japanese-American; she was talkative and bubbly, a great storyteller, a leader of fun songs, never shy, and always attentive to our needs as young adults. I was enraptured by such a novel Sansei woman. As a pastor's wife, she took over as advisor for our Junior MYF (Methodist Youth Fellowship). The first thing she did was to introduce a curriculum—a booklet with youth stories and themes to read and discuss.

At one of our first MYF meetings, Dorothy said that each of us would take turns leading the discussion after each chapter and then named names: "Harriet, you are in charge of discussion for Chapter One, Julia for Chapter Two...."

I was appalled and terrified because I had never led a discussion group in my life. I begged to be let off the hook, and I thought perhaps I could feign illness and not show up.

But Dorothy would have none of that. She would not take "No" for an answer from anyone. We enjoyed the games and singing and food, and one-by-one, we put our toes into this very chilly water of "leadership."

Much to our surprise, we realized that the water was not as chilly as we had thought. After the first experience, being a discussion leader became easier and easier with more and more practice. I needed to get out of my shell at a time when the demands of peer pressure and popularity were coming to the forefront of my young life. Dorothy was the mentor who guided so many of us in the junior MYF through those crucial years. We remain indebted to this unusual Sansei woman, who presently lives in Medford, Oregon, and shares many e-mail tidbits with us on a regular basis, at the age of ninety.

Dorothy not only made me move past my shyness into being involved and interested in serving others, but she opened my eyes to the situation of the Japanese in the United States' recent past by sharing her stories about her years spent in a Japanese concentration camp during World War II. We in Hawai'i had been insulated from the incarceration experience because only a few adult leaders were taken from Hawai'i and put into the camps, whereas 120,000 Japanese who lived on the West Coast of the United States, most of whom were American citizens—men, women, and children—were imprisoned in one of ten camps.

Dorothy told us how she had been an honor student in her senior year at Tulare Union High School, in Tulare, California. However, she could not celebrate graduation and receive her hard-earned honor because of Executive Order 9066, proclaimed by President Franklin Delano Roosevelt on February 19, 1942.

Dorothy and her family were ordered to pack only what each person could carry and report to the Fresno Fairgrounds, where they were housed in converted horse stalls. From there, the Ichinaga family traveled in a very old train with armed guards to Jerome, Arkansas. The Jerome camp eventually housed around 16,000 Japanese-Americans. A PBS documentary film, *Time of Fear*, produced in 2004, told the story of the Jerome camp and a similar camp in nearby Rohwer, Arkansas.

This story did not hit home for me at first because I had not yet seen the photos taken of the women and children boarding buses and trains, each with numbers hanging from their necks. When I was first introduced to the photo display of Executive Order 9066 as a graduate student in California, a torrent of tears streamed forth. I could not believe that the youth who looked like me were being treated like cattle, wearing large prison numbers.

My best friends, Mary Tomita and Miya Okawara of Oakland and San Francisco, were part of the movement to gain an apology from the U.S. Congress for the imprisonment, and also $25,000 per person in redress funds for taking away the civil rights of a whole group of people just because they were Japanese. I joined in the movement through Sycamore Congregational Church in El Cerrito, and our resolution, which started at the local church level, moved through all the necessary hoops finally to reach the General Assembly of the United Church of Christ. There on the floor of the General Synod, Miya Okawara shared her personal story and the story of her people in such a powerful way that the delegates voted unanimously to support the Resolution calling for an Apology and for Redress. This was the first national church resolution calling for monetary redress, since many other denominational resolutions were inclined to talk about "Apology," but not about monetary redress.

Readers in Hawai'i may want further elaboration about the Japanese leadership who were imprisoned first in local camps and then moved to one of the camps on the continental United States. Even though 1,200-1,800 Japanese leaders from Hawai'i were imprisoned, the majority of us who were farm workers and children of farm workers were not affected by this call for incarceration. At the time of Executive Order 9066, the Japanese people numbered 150,000 in Hawai'i. Thus, around .009 percent of the Hawaiian Japanese were incarcerated. More than 95 percent of the Japanese-Americans on the West Coast were put in concentration camps.

As a graduate student in the School of Social Work at UC-Berkeley, I raised my hand when the topic of the mass incarceration of Japanese-Americans on the West Coast was mentioned by the professor. I asked why Japanese in Hawai'i, who lived closer to Japan, were not incarcerated for "security" reasons, while West Coast Japanese were all told to report to holding centers before being shipped off to the interior of the country as prisoners of the U.S.

The answer my professor gave was astounding and shocking: the Japanese from the West Coast were imprisoned for their own "security." Otherwise, they would be beaten by civilians who were angry at the Japanese people living in their midst because of what had happened at Pearl Harbor.

I could not believe what I was hearing, especially from as progressive an institution as the University of California in Berkeley. I tried to set the record straight by explaining that my parents and I had not been incarcerated because we were "cheap labor" in the sugar and pineapple fields of Hawai'i and the entire Hawaiian economy would have been devastated if 150,000 cheap laborers were shipped to the continental prisons.

Sure enough, when I later did research on the topic of why Hawaiian Japanese were not incarcerated en masse, there was mention at Wikipedia that the "productivity" of the Hawaiian economy would have been affected negatively. Productivity—a wonderful euphemism for cheap farm labor on the Hawaiian plantations—was the real reason why I did not end up in a concentration camp.

Since the Japanese in California were responsible for 95 percent of the vegetable-farming production when World War II began, the greedy neighbors and residents of California used muckraking journalism to incite fear and anger at the successful Japanese farmers, who owned land in the name of their children. And when one looks at the result of the incarceration, the truth is that millions of dollars were lost by the Japanese farmers and businessmen because their lands and businesses were mostly confiscated. Greed, jealousy, and racism were at the root of Executive Order 9066.

It is ironic that the Japanese in Hawai'i actually somewhat improved their situation during the war years. Because so many men left the islands to go to war, many positions were left open for non-English-speaking but productive workers to be hired from the plantations.

My father was one of those who benefited from the labor scarcity; he became a security guard at the Wahiawa water tower, a much easier job than toiling for ten hours under the hot sun in a sugarcane field.

Another way we benefited was through the need for flowers for the newly-fallen Hawaiian soldiers. My mother knew how to raise dahlias and our dahlias in Wahiawa grew to a diameter of about twelve inches. These huge dahlias became famous as the Matsui dahlia, an item in great demand during the war years.

As time went on, the dahlias grew smaller and smaller. It finally dawned on my mother and father that the red dirt of Wahiawa was a rich bed of naturally composted soil from the trees and shrubs that grew wild in the area before our garden was built. The natural rich soil dissipated over the years, and unfortunately, the Matsui dahlia never entered the *Guinness Book of World Records*.

My mentor, Dorothy Ichinaga, taught me compassion training and joy in living, and she also taught me about racism through her personal story about being put in a concentration camp as an eighteen-year-old. She opened my eyes, and I have never closed them since.

Jumping Jacks and Public Education

Despite the racism existing within the public school system at that time, I feel a deep sense of gratitude when I reflect back upon my student days at Wahiawa Elementary and Leilehua High School. We had some of the most caring teachers. I wonder sometimes whether it had to do with the clean mountain air and the cool weather, where no air conditioner was ever needed. To be real, there were probably two or three teachers who had the reputation for being "mean and uncaring," but most of the teachers were wonderful.

So many notable people have come out of our Wahiawa public school system…a famous magician, a famous chef, a chief justice of the Hawai'i Supreme Court, a bishop of the United Methodist Church, and many others.

Because we were always seated alphabetically, I had as my seatmate through our elementary years, Ronald Moon, who would one day serve as the chief justice in our Hawai'i court system. I am sure we were friends for the most part, but I remember one day when I stabbed Ronald Moon in the wrist with my pencil.

Why would I want to stab a fellow student? I faintly recall it being a test day in sixth grade when I noticed his wandering eyes. Fortunately, in 1951, schools did not have a "no tolerance policy" for any acts of violence. Otherwise, I would have been hauled off to the police station for questioning and discipline.

Since lead is poisonous, I could barely sleep that night from worrying that I had put poison into Ronald's bloodstream. When he arrived at school the next morning looking chipper, I was much relieved. Thus I learned a valuable lesson—a sharp pencil is a tool for paper and not an instrument to be used to settle a score.

My appreciation for good teachers includes my eighth grade physical education instructor. She drilled into my mind that "100 jumping jacks a day will keep the doctor away." Thus I have faithfully done my jumping jacks since eighth grade until today. I, in turn, have tried to teach that maxim to all my friends in the hopes that we can all be healthier. Hopefully, many of the millions of readers out there will begin to form the "jumping jack" habit and doctors will have to find a new occupation.

The highest accolade goes to my eleventh grade English teacher, Mrs. Hoshibata. Learning from her how to diagram long and complex sentences was a challenge. And diagramming President Lincoln's *The Gettysburg Address* was a moving, as well as challenging, experience. Even more memorable was reading the short story "The Devil and Daniel Webster" by Stephen Vincent Benet. So much of what we learned in English often focused on ethical/spiritual values. No wonder Mrs. Hoshibata's son, Robert, became a bishop of the United Methodist Church, respected highly for his courageous stance on many justice issues.

Our graduating class of 1958 is very fortunate because we have classmates who are willing to commit time and energy into bringing our school 'ohana together every five years or so. Now that we are beginning to lose some of our classmates via the aging process, a small core of dedicated persons bring us together every other year, led by chair Pauline (Ishii) Kamisato. It will be a sad day indeed if Pauline ever retires from such a worthy enterprise.

Public education deserves more support from the general population. Like universal health care, quality universal education will be the hallmark of the future. Already this is happening with the public funding of preschools in Hawai'i, thanks to courageous and visionary politicians like Hawaii's House of Representatives member Roy Takumi of Pearl City. I have held many a sign for Roy because we learned in school that every vote does count. Indeed, in one election, Roy won by as few votes as what one could count on one hand. Because of his commitment to public education, he is one of only a few politicians who chose to send all of his children to public school even if he could afford private schools for them. "Walking the talk" is a hard and courageous act.

Roger and I sent our son Bob to public schools from kindergarten through San Francisco State University because of our commitment to public education and also because we knew he was getting a solid education, and at the same time, making many friends from all races and backgrounds as well. We also made sure that Bob's education was "solid" by talking to his teachers as needed. In ninth grade, for example, Bob came home with a "D" in Spanish. Roger and I made an appointment with the teacher, Ms. Ramirez, to discover the root of the problem. Because his parents showed interest in his studies, Bob studied harder and thus was able to move from a D to a C or maybe even a B-.

Once we stop spending so much money for military bases all over the world (one source cites 1,000 or more U.S. bases in foreign countries), state-funded education, especially colleges and universities, will hopefully become affordable again.

50th Anniversary Reunion: Trinidad Orosco, Gloriana Virgeniza, Pauline Ishii, Julia Matsui, Annette Akimoto.

50th Anniversary Reunion: Annette Akimoto, Julia Matsui, Ernest Tanji, Eleanor Ota, Roy Ogasawara.

Anthony Consillio photo

Ronald MOON

>> For 17 years, Ronald Moon served as Hawaii's Chief Justice, and for his more than 30 years of work serving the state and its people, the Kapolei judiciary complex has been named "Ronald T. Y. Moon Judiciary Complex" and its courthouse, "Ronald T.Y. Moon Courthouse." In fact, Moon has the distinction of being the first Korean-American to be chief justice of any Supreme Court in the United States.

Moon, who was featured on *MidWeek*'s cover Dec. 30, 1998, said hello to retirement three years ago and decided he would take six months off and do virtually nothing.

"I told myself I would study the lay of the land and determine what I would like to do," he explains.

However, six months after retirement, Moon fell off a ladder going up to his roof and broke his back.

"I had what they call a compression fracture," he says. "The vertebrae were crushed together. I was not able to walk for a long time, and I didn't know if I was going to walk again."

But thanks to the wonders of modern medicine and the staff at The Queen's Medical Center and REHAB hospital, as well as his daughter Julie Moon-Franklin (owner of Moon's Physical Therapy) and sons Scott Moon (director of radiation oncology operations at Queen's) and Ron Moon Jr. (a physician in Alabama), he is up and running.

Now that he's back on his feet, Moon has been involved in many board activities. He sits on the board for his alma mater Mid-Pacific Institute, as well as Saint Louis High School, Wahiawa United Church of Christ (on the Board of Deacons) and Kick Start Karate with Lee Donohue (as the vice president of the board).

Most recently, he agreed to sit on the board of Ohana Pacific Bank, which opened a new branch last month in Kalihi.

"It gives me the opportunity to ... serve the public," Moon says. "I believe that being with a bank, especially a small bank like this, that initially started focusing on the Korean population and is looking to spread its wings to other ethnic groups ... helps to serve the public to help them with their finances.

"I'm very happy to be here."

There's no doubt that Moon is enjoying retirement, and he seems to be just as busy as ever.

He is eager to add that his wife Stella has been instrumental in assisting him with his career.

"She has been my sounding board throughout the years — my best critic, motivator, guide and counsel," he adds. "And when I was incapacitated after breaking my back three years ago, she trained and acquired skills to be the ultimate caregiver — truly an unbelievable wife and best friend."

—*Nicole Kato*

---

1 Printed with the permission of the *Honolulu Star Advertiser.*

Part Two

GROWING BRANCHES
AND BUDS

"A freedom of choice
Is given to everyone
Man can thus create
Either a heaven or a hell,
According to his heart.

Let us be aware
That the true source of sorrow
Or joy in our lives
Is always something
We create by our own hands."

— Mokichi Okada

Being Okinawan

All of us, at one time or another, have had a little voice speak to us from the depths of our being. I've always wondered where the words of wisdom come from. Recently, I've concluded that some of these gems are imbedded in our genes, thanks to our ancestors.

My first awareness of what was unique about being Okinawan came from my mother. Okinawans have a shamanist tradition, and I saw my mother as a kind of shaman. She knew how to fix a sprained foot with "yama imo" (root plant), flour, ginger, and water made into a paste and bandaged around one's foot. Amazingly, in one day, the sprain would be gone. Healing concoctions seemed to come from within her body knowledge. My sister and I were often amazed at the seemingly everyday miracles emanating from someone who had no schooling beyond eighth grade.

It was not until graduate school in California that I began learning about the history of Okinawa. As a child, I knew that Okinawans were different because Japanese children called us names like "buta kau kau" (pig eater). And I was darker and had more hair than my Japanese counterparts. The name "blackie" was also often used as a taunt. However, since my father was from Hiroshima, many of our dealings were with the Japanese community.

Once in awhile, my mother would meet a fellow Okinawan and start speaking in "Uchina Guchi," a language independent from Japanese. My mother seemed to love speaking the language because it must have reminded her of her village and her childhood years. Okinawa was originally known as Ryuchoo or the Ryukyu Islands, and the group of islands had once had its own king, religion, language, and own unique dances, games, music, and food.

In 1609, the Shimazu clan of Satsuma invaded Okinawa. At the same time, the ruler of Okinawa ordered his people not to fight back. Instead, he told the people that "Life is a treasure." This history resonates with me because when the U.S. invaded Hawai'i with military forces in 1893, Queen Lili'uokalani told her people not to fight back because life was precious and no blood was to be shed. The similarities between the U.S. occupation of Hawai'i and Japan's occupation of Okinawa have so many similarities.

After the invasion by the Shimazu clan, Okinawa became a tributary to Japan for many years and officially became a prefecture of Japan in 1876. The Okinawan language and culture were banned by the Japanese government in an attempt to "assimilate" Okinawans into becoming Japanese. Fortunately, the Okinawan people persisted in maintaining their own identity and a new renaissance period seems to have begun in recent years with the revival of "uchina guchi" in some of the schools and universities.

Much of the battle between the U.S. and Japan in World War II took place in Micronesia and Okinawa, and millions of civilians died in the crossfire between these two major powers. One fourth of the Okinawan civilian population died in the Battle of Okinawa. The U.S. military took home many of the treasures that soldiers found as they searched homes and museums. And the story goes that the Okinawan king's crown was taken by someone in the U.S. military during Okinawa's occupation. When the crown is found and returned to the Okinawan people, it is the dream and hope of the Okinawan people that their sovereignty will be restored and Okinawa will be free of any super power. This story of hope was shared with me by Professor Ron Nakasone, a Buddhist priest and professor at the Graduate Theological Union in Berkeley.

Much of my education about being Okinawan came by way of Professor Nakasone, whom I worked with when I served as the director of the Pacific and Asian American Center for Theologies and Strategies (PACTS) at the Pacific School of Religion and the Graduate Theological Union from 1987 to 1995. Since PACTS was an interfaith theological body in the two schools, our board of directors consisted of people from different religions and Professor Nakasone served as the chair of PACTS for many years. In 1996, Professor Nakasone edited a book, *Reflections on the Okinawan Experience: Essays Commemorating 100 years of Okinawan Immigration* (Dharma Cloud Publishers). Much of my intellectual understanding of "being Okinawan" comes from this book. The chapter titles show the "richness" of Okinawan culture and history: Okinawan Textiles; Okinawan Household Shrines; Okinawan Music and Dance; Yanagi Soetsu and the Pure Land of Beauty; Okinawan Issei Identity; Survival and Determination; Politics of Okinawan Identity: Forgetting, Recovery, and Empowerment; Higa Tooki and His Time. Many of the stories come with illustrations of such terms as: picture bride, ceramic dish, shisaa (a statue of a mythological Okinawan creature), Okinawan trading ship, and "butchidan" (family worship center).

Okinawans believe that women are gifted with spiritual powers superior to those of men. Thus, the female assumes the role of the spiritual patron. The male in turn guides and protects the woman in secular affairs. Two principal figures of Okinawan religion are the "kaminchu" (priestess) and the "yuta" (shaman). The kaminchu is a hereditary position and refers to the priestess in charge of the religious rites associated with the larger community. The yuta is believed to possess powers of clairvoyance and also has the ability to communicate with the spirit world.

One of my favorite Okinawan stories was told to me by a historian friend concerning New Year's Day. On the first day of the New Year, the King of Okinawa was required to dress as a woman in order to enter the sacred area where the priestess was in charge of the holy ritual. He did this because only women were allowed into this sacred space.

I recently contacted a yuta who lives in Hawai'i to ask whether I should pursue an unresolved land issue in Kita-Nakagusuku—seventeen parcels of land that would have belonged to my mother in Okinawa—if she had acted in a timely manner. The yuta's advice was to pursue the matter because it was the death wish of my mother. Hopefully, I will receive more guidance and assistance in the near future.

I tend to identify with my Okinawan heritage more than with my other identities as Japanese or U.S. North American because Okinawans are oppressed by both the U.S. and Japan, as seen in the U.S. base issue. Later in the book, I have shown this by attaching a petition from the people of Okinawa to the U.S/Japan requesting removal of the U.S. bases.

For those interested in more information about Okinawa, I recommend viewing online the short community-based documentary film *Typhoon of Steel*. It explores through touching interviews the lives of two Okinawan-American Kibei Nisei who served in the U.S. military as linguists in the Battle of

Okinawa during World War II. While Japanese-Americans were being placed in U.S. concentration camps, these men risked their lives to prove their loyalty to America. Born in the U.S. and raised in Okinawa, their cultural and linguistic skills were a tactical asset to the military. But emotions ran high as they returned to their homeland to save their own families, witness civilian casualties, and see their homeland devastated by war. The video is available at: http://vimeo.com/43881807

You can also see a video of me made by the *Washington Post* in July, 2010, sharing what it means to me to be an Okinawan-American at http://vimeo.com/16602693

Recently, I've become interested in the movement to revitalize the Okinawan language among those in Hawai'i of Okinawan descent. The Okinawan community in Hawai'i is mobilizing at this time to figure out ways to revitalize the Okinawan language. Below is an announcement for a recent presentation about this topic.

Gusuuyo Chuuganabira! (Hello)

This is an announcement and reminder for our monthly Gakumun Kai, Okinawa Cultural Presentation.

THIS SUNDAY, FEBRUARY 2, 12 P.M. JIKOEN

TOPIC: OKINAWAN LANGUAGE ENDANGERMENT AND REVITALIZATION & HOW LANGUAGE IS CONNECTED TO CULTURE AND IDENTITY

We will be discussing the endangerment of Okinawan language and what's being done about revitalization. We will also present on how language is directly connected to Okinawan culture and identity.

Within only 60 yrs, the language of our ancestors has gone from almost 100% to 5%. We will see why this is the case and look at what is being done to revitalize. However, we must realize that the window is closing for our resources to be tapped into.

We are lucky to be living here in Hawai'i in a time when the Hawaiian language is beginning to thrive. The Hawaiian language was also once at where we are now, but through their aggressive work and rebuilding of their foundations, language is not only taught, but it lives in the work, play, music, dances and hearts of thousands of Hawaiians and non Hawaiians. Come and listen to how and why this is a success.

Please take time to come and listen and discuss about this very important issue facing Okinawa. If you are a performing artist participating in dance or music, this topic is one that you should come and hear.

Please share with your friends and relatives and bring them with you. It is free and open to the public.

Yutasarugutu Unigeesabira! (Until the Next Time)

If you are interesting in learning the Okinawan language, a great place to start is at http://www.sanshinshop.com/Okinawan_Language.html. This website includes a clear description of the basics of the Okinawan language and also has several videos demonstrating how the language sounds and various beginning expressions you can learn.

The loss of our cultural identity, language, and ethnic origin is always tragic. I encourage people to educate themselves on their family heritage and ethnic backgrounds, whether they are Hawaiian, Okinawan, Japanese, or Finnish, English, Dutch, German, Egyptian, Ethiopian, Chinese, Russian, Indian, or any other identity. Knowing and appreciating where we come from gives us strength and understanding for facing the future.

A Love Story

In the summer of 1968, my friend Josie set me up on a blind double date. She was a member of the First United Methodist Church of Oakland, California where I served as the full-time director of Christian education. Josie was single also, so she invited her friend Roger as her date and asked Roger's best friend, Oscar, to be my date.

Dinner was at a tiny restaurant famous for its hot pot specialties, located in neighboring Berkeley. We enjoyed putting various vegetables and meat into the steaming pot and made sure we used our chopsticks to pick up the vegetables from the pot while they were still crunchy and not overcooked.

After dinner, Josie suggested that we go bowling. I had never bowled so I was not too enthusiastic, but I went along with the plan. I noticed that Oscar was very shy and not saying much, while Roger was effervescent and eager to teach me how to bowl; he even offered me his sweater when we walked outside into a cool evening. Therefore, when the phone rang the next morning, I had a hunch that it was Roger on the other end—and my hunch was correct.

Roger had arrived from the Philippines two years prior and was working on his Ph.D. in physics at the University of California, Berkeley, under a Rockefeller grant. I already had a special male friend of sorts who lived in the Sacramento area, about 120 miles away. I was doubting whether I should have gone on that blind double date after all.

When I finally told Roger at the end of summer about my special friend, he took me outside to look at the star-lit skies. He pointed to a shooting star and proclaimed that my Sacramento friend was like the shooting star—a "dead" star traveling through space. I was still not convinced, so I decided I needed time and space to check what my heart was ultimately saying.

By some synchronicity, an invitation unexpectedly arrived from the senior pastor of the First Methodist Church of Sacramento offering me a full-time position there as Minister of Youth. I immediately accepted and felt I had made the right decision. Actually, I was running away from the idea of marriage. Having enjoyed my independence ever since I left home, I was sure that the best option for me was singlehood, since I enjoyed my work and wanted to see as many places in the world as possible before settling down.

However, scientists like Roger never give up on their complicated mathematical formulations—or a complicated relationship situation. I was amazed that he could turn my "No's" into "Yes's." The final showdown arrived one evening when I informed Roger over the phone that I had chosen not to see him anymore. Sadly, he commented that he had just purchased a Picasso poster called "Guernica" at a Berkeley art shop because he knew I was a peace activist. Roger announced that he was coming over to present the poster as a farewell present.

Thirty minutes later, he was standing on my dimly-lit porch looking extremely forlorn. My heart melted and I made a complete U-turn. So we started to date again, and the first movie we saw after the U-turn was *Gone with the Wind*, a wonderfully complicated love story. Once again, under a brightly-lit sky in the Berkeley Hills, Roger said he was going to ask me a hypothetical question: if he were to ask me to marry him, would I consider it? This time my answer was a definite "Yes."

Knowing that my mother would be upset because Roger was a Filipino, I decided to drive down a few days prior to Thanksgiving to prepare my parents for the news. A lot of prejudice existed in the Japanese community in Hawai'i against Filipino men because they were the newest immigrants who came to work on the sugar and pineapple plantations. And as the newest immigrants, who arrived without wives and were the first to be fired during economic down times, unemployed Filipino men hung around pool halls and often whistled at single girls. Thus, the men were stereotyped as lazy, poor, and without a bright future.

My mother brought this prejudice with her to California, where she and my father lived with my sister near Los Angeles.

When I brought "white" male friends to the house, my mother was pleased because in her way of thinking, "white" meant climbing up the social and economic ladders, whereas Filipino men were seen as a downward climb. My mother was a very strong Okinawan woman, so I wasn't sure how she would express her displeasure.

Sure enough, once I shared the news with my parents that Roger and I were engaged and that he would be arriving the day before Thanksgiving to meet them, my mother took to her bed and refused to get up to eat or do anything. My father was always happy and genial, so he had no objections to a Filipino son-in-law, especially since he had worked side-by-side with Filipinos as farmworkers in the Waipahu and Kauai sugarcane fields.

Since my mother was a strong Christian, I decided to share verses from the Bible as she determinedly lay in her bed. I was hoping that her Christian belief in compassion and the need to follow in the footsteps of Jesus could somehow overcome her personal and communal prejudices. However, she kept saying she would not be able to face her friends and relatives back in Hawai'i. Somehow, what friends back home would think of our family once they heard the news was upsetting her more than anything else. I gave up on reading Bible verses and just prayed for the best.

The moment arrived when the doorbell rang and Roger was at the door. I looked at my mom and quietly reminded her that the doorbell was ringing. Her Okinawan culture of "hospitality to all visitors" was stronger than her prejudice at that moment. I truly think extravagant hospitality is wired into the genes of the Okinawan people.

When my mother opened the door, she was surprised to be greeted with, "Okāsan," which means "Mother" in Japanese. Mother melted completely at hearing "Okāsan" and prejudice was healed with that one word of endearment and love.

Julia sewed her own gown.

The Phillippine Connection

When I married Rogelio (Roger) Estrella on June 22, 1968, in Oakland, California, a little pebble was thrown into the large Pacific Ocean and the circles grew larger and larger as our life together expanded and the waters of the San Francisco Bay area reached the shores of the Philippines.

While teaching physics at the University of the Philippines, Roger was awarded a full scholarship to pursue a doctorate in physics at the University of California in Berkeley. Arriving in Berkeley in the fall of 1967, he joined a group of other Rockefeller grantees studying in different fields at the Berkeley campus. But as soon as the Rockefeller scholarship office heard of Roger's marriage, the grant was immediately terminated. Rockefeller felt that Roger would not return to teach at the University of the Philippines if he married a U.S. citizen. However, Roger was always committed to return and teach someday at U.P. until President Marcos of the Philippines declared martial law. At that point, the physics department at the university was a hotbed of activism against martial law; therefore, many of the physics professors ended up being arrested by Marcos' military. Therefore, Roger's friends asked him to remain in the Bay area to gain support from prominent physicists in the U.S. to call for the release of the prisoners. Roger was indeed able to obtain the signatures of several Nobel physicists from Berkeley to call for the release of their fellow physicists in the Philippines. The campaign seemed to have worked since many of them were released and went back to teach again even during the martial law years. Meanwhile, with Roger no longer having the grant funding, it became our joint task to find work in order to pay for the huge "out of state" tuition.

Life was hectic but enjoyable, especially with the arrival of our son Robert into our lives on March 20, 1969.

Because we wanted Bob to grow up with Asian values, we took regular trips to the Philippines to expose him to his extended family. On these visits, I especially loved the way children and youth showed their respect every morning to older siblings and to their parents and older relatives living in the household.

Despite the poverty we saw in Roger's family's neighborhood in Project 2, Quezon City, a vibrancy and enjoyment of life seemed to exist there that was unique to Filipino culture in the Philippines, and we witnessed it among all our relatives, rich and poor alike.

The relatives in the countryside, the barrios, were very poor, and those in urban areas were middle class since the head of the household (Roger's brother-in-law) was a physician who had his clinic attached to his home. Dr. Lamasan's daughter and family moved to eastern Canada and his son and family moved to the Vancouver area. The remaining two daughters— Carol and Sheila—still live in the house where they grew up— the one Bob and I stay at whenever we visit the Philippines. I correspond with Carol and Sheila by e-mail on a regular basis, thus keeping our bonds to the Philippines fresh.

Roger's older brother had married into the extended family of Diosdado Macapagal, who served as the ninth President of the Philippines from 1961 to 1965. Diosdado's daughter, Gloria Macapagal-Arroyo, served as the fourteenth President of the Philippines from 2001 to 2010. On one of our visits to the Philippines, we received an invitation to have dinner with Diosdado Macapagal at his home in Forbes Park, an exclusive gated residential area. The reason for the invitation, we discovered as the evening wore on, was to find out how the anti-martial law work (organizing against dictator president Marcos) was progressing in northern California. Roger and I were very active in the anti-martial law movement in the Bay area; thus our dinner event turned out to be a sharing of information on the anti-martial law movement both in the Bay area and in the Philippines. It was a fun evening with the children playing in the background.

Our son Bob probably does not remember this visit to the former President of the Philippines. I think he was more awed at meeting the head of the Director of Tourism in the Philippines since he arranged for special cars to take us to some famous tourist spots. Manila traffic would melt away as a special siren opened up a path for our caravan of cars…. Bob must have felt like President Obama's children visiting snow cone shops in Honolulu with all traffic giving way to their entourage.

Lest I give the wrong impression of our visits to the Philippines, most of Roger's relatives were very poor and we learned more from our grassroots relatives who took the time to introduce us to important values of family and community. We also arranged for Roger, Bob, and me to have dental work done while in the Philippines—it was more affordable there than in the U.S.

When Bob graduated from Berkeley High School in 1987, his graduation gift was a roundtrip ticket to the Philippines with his pastor Rev. Ben Wu of Sycamore Congregational Church. When some of our Filipino friends heard that the two were coming to "experience" the Philippines, they arranged for visits in the countryside to meet with peasants, fishermen, and church people in Christian-based communities. Dangers of martial law were still present everywhere. One night, Bob and Ben were awakened in the middle of the night while staying with a Catholic-based community in the countryside; they were told to leave immediately before military men roaming the area showed up at their doorsteps. Those were dangerous days for Christian communities, led by activist priests who were fighting for the civil and human rights of the common people. Sadly, even with martial law gone today, there are stories of human rights abuses in the countryside, especially for workers and laborers. The need for vigilance to overcome violence with plowshares instead of swords continues.

This past Christmas, I wrote to Carol and Sheila, Roger's nieces in the Philippines, who head up the Estrella household at 35 Marang, Project 2 in Quirino. Many of the family members have moved to Canada or to California, so the large extended family in Quezon City has become a smaller core of nieces, nephews, and cousins. Hopefully, Bob and I will be able to travel to the Philippines in 2014 to renew our ties with our 'ohana there. The energy in the Philippines is very palpable and uplifting—we have much to learn from our relatives overseas.

Lamasan family in Quezon City, Philippines.

Julia, January Cano Liddell, Sam Liddell, Nancy Willimek.
January Cano is part of our Philippine connection in Hawai'i.

The Best Birthday Gift

Many of us born on the day after Christmas never see a birthday party—the traditional kind with plenty of friends, games, balloons, and a birthday cake with candles. When I tell my friends of this unfortunate circumstance, one or two will remember to invite me out to have lunch or dinner with them.

One such friend was June Shimokawa, director of the American Friends Service Committee (AFSC) in Honolulu for many years. About eight years ago, June treated me to a lovely lunch at a small "hole in the wall" eating establishment. June always supported local mom-and-pop restaurants and local farmers' markets…..anything "local" was her passion. As we were engaged in a deep conversation about our hopes for the new year, she pulled out a package and said, "Happy Birthday."

Enclosed in the package was the best birthday present I have ever received. It was an issue of *YES* magazine published in Bainbridge Island, Washington. When I returned home, I read my birthday present from cover to cover and my spirit soared. *YES* was full of wonderful stories from ordinary people engaged in changing the world one step at a time. I was instantly addicted to the magazine and subscribed immediately. When *YES* offered back copies, I ordered all of them. I was delighted to hear that *YES* was the 2013 winner of the UTNE Media Award for General Excellence—a big recognition for a nonprofit, independent, subscriber-supported magazine.

As I sit here reading the Fall 2013 issue, my day is uplifted by reading about "How One Town Is Saving Its Teens." Then to hold me "accountable" for what I can do now to make a difference, there is a commentary titled, "Climate Change: One Thing You Can Do Right Now, Alumni." It told of how Laurent Dalaz, an alumnus of Williams College, wrote a check to his alma mater and respectfully informed the college that until it divested its holdings in the fossil fuel industry—coal, oil, tar sands, and fracked natural gas—he would not donate another cent. I also learned from the commentary that colleges care a great deal about the percentage of their alumni who give—indeed, their public ratings rest, in part, on this criterion.

Since the last paragraph of the commentary is what finally moved me to action, I am sharing those words with you:

> In the end, what message do we choose to give the next generation? What will we say to them as the storms grow fiercer, the droughts longer, the waters higher? That "we just didn't know?" Or that we woke up too late? We know what to do right now. There are many actions we can take to make a difference. This is one. Take it now. Tell your alumni organization, your development director, and your college president that you will resume giving when they divest of all holdings in fossil fuel extraction and production.

While reading the challenge, I recalled the demonstration I attended at University Hall in Berkeley, calling upon the Board of Regents of the UC system, to make a decision to divest from South Africa. I was a second year master's degree student in the School of Social Welfare, and I was working as an aide to Ying Lee, the first Asian American to be elected to the Berkeley City Council. The leaders of the demonstration called for those who were willing to be arrested—in an act of civil disobedience—to step forward to block the building entrance and prevent the regents from entering the building. Councilwoman Ying looked at me and said, "Julia, you and I need to get arrested. Look, there are only blacks and whites stepping forward, and we are the only Asians here." With that statement, she gave me a gentle push toward the entrance. And we were arrested with around 100 other students that day who decided to take a stand against apartheid. That was the beginning of my training in what I like to call "civil obedience"—doing what is right for humanity.

I was also recently impressed by a January 2014 article in *YES* about the Empathy Library by Roman Krznaric. The Empathy Library is a digital archive that allows people to select the books, movies, and other types of media that allow us to share information and learn from one another. Here is a short excerpt from the article titled "How a Library with No Books Could Change the Way We Read (And Bring Us Closer Together)":

> How does the Empathy Library actually work? Although it doesn't contain items to borrow or view, there are reviews and ratings of over 100 books such as Toni Morrison's *The Bluest Eye* and George Orwell's *Down and Out in Paris and London*, alongside movies like *Gandhi* and *Avatar*. The library collection also includes dozens of fantastic books and films for children and teens. Visitors can search the collection and view Top Ten Charts, and join up to add their own favorite items and comment on others.

By coincidence, the Fall 2013 issue of *YES* had a beautiful full-page color photo of Nelson Mandela taken by photographer Jane Feldman on Mandela's 2005 visit to Riverside Church on page 12 with a story titled "An Uncommon View." The Fall Issue came off the press in September, preceding Mandela's passing in December. My son, Bob, was one of the first in our neck of the woods to put a tribute to Mandela on his Facebook page when the news came to Hawai'i. It brought to mind that day when Roger, Bob, and I went to hear Mandela speak at the Oakland Stadium, soon after his release from prison. One could hear a pin drop in that huge stadium packed to overflowing. It was the only time I have felt the instantaneous unity of all peoples of color as hushed silence descended upon the crowd of thousands and Mandela walked on to that stage. As people stood up weeping for joy, I thought to myself, "This is heaven on earth."

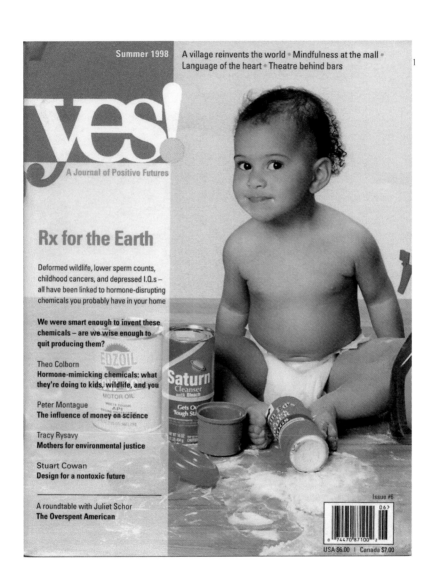

Mary and Miya: A Poetic Tribute

Knock, knock, knock. A strange woman at the door.
"Who are you?"
"I'm Mary Tomita from Sycamore Church,
Sent to ask if you can be our Christian ed. director."
"Please come in…."

Thus began thirty-eight years of escapades with a fun-loving, witty, outspoken Mary. Although separated by twenty-two years, we were both Nisei, raised by Issei parents and understood the nuances of growing up Nisei in America.

Racism, sexism, and classism were our favorite topics at lunches and dinners. Together with Miya Okawara, the editor of our PAAM newsletter.

Nothing can replace the simple lunches of misoshiru, rice, and tsukemono at Mary's. With her beloved dog, Kaiki, at her side. I thought, "Heaven must be like this."

Now Mary and Miya are in heaven, having Japanese food together with other loved ones; with "Kaiki" at their side.

I miss my comfort food and constant companions,
And yet they are with me daily,
With their encouraging words, their smiles, and their prodding. What more can anyone ask for?

Knock, knock, knock.
"Who are you?"

Third PAAM Conference   Pacific Palisades   Southern, CA.
1st Row--Ron Fujiyoshi, Yoshi Kaneda, Mary Tomita, Mary Terada, Sachi Fujita,
Tom Fujita, Yuri Kaneda, X, Karl Fung, Eugenia Fung, Julia Nakamura, Kiku Uno,
Arthur Kobayashi, X. 2nd Row--Franklin Chan, Julia Estrella, X, Angel Taglacup,
Miya Okawara, Ken Katahira, Sr., David Unoura, Mary Unoura, Setsuko Kaneda,
Marilyn Moore, George Nishimoto, X. 3rd Row--Terry Terada, Franklin Odo, Frank
Chong, Goldrino Balatico, Tyrone Reinhardt, David Hirano, Henry Aarona, Jr.,
Jimmy Terada, X, X, Ken Katahira, Jr.

Julia of Berkeley, Alfonso Roman of Puerto Rico,
Sumi and Rev. Ben Wu.

Invisible Institutional Racism

Institutional racism is often invisible to people in power. Because of their power privilege, people who are the decision-makers often act without thinking about the consequences of their actions.

For example, I was asked by the national body of the United Church of Christ to serve on a blue-ribbon committee on economic justice, which was mandated by the General Synod to implement a pronouncement on the topic. I was chastised for missing a number of meetings and a statement was made that people of color were put on important committees but did not have a good attendance record. Therefore, I took it upon myself to do some research on why people of color were often absent at the table.

I discovered, in the process of asking questions, that dates for the meetings were set first by asking "important" people for available dates. In other words, those individuals deemed powerful—or "important"—chose the dates, and then the people of color who were deemed not as powerful or important were told to show up on those dates picked by the "important" people. I remember that I was unable to attend one of the meetings because my Board of Directors of the Pacific and Asian American Center for Theologies and Strategies (PACTS) also met on the dates chosen.

Not once were all committee members sent a questionnaire asking which dates were best according to their work schedules. Instead, one group was asked for its availability.

Another group, usually those representing racial or ethnic constituencies, was told just to show up on the dates chosen by the first group. No wonder that often the second group—which had not been consulted—did not show up because of schedule conflicts.

Fortunately, I had just attended a workshop on invisible institutional racism sponsored by the California state library system. It sponsored the workshop because libraries in neighborhoods that had changed from a predominantly white population to one of people of color were no longer being fully utilized, and the result was that community libraries were dying. Through the training, it became clear that the libraries were dying because the delivery of service to the community had not changed to be culturally appropriate to the new residents. The instructor focused on the fact that when institutional racism happens, the person who can recognize the racism must point it out while the incident is happening.

Thanks to that training, I was immediately able to point out to the staff of the UCC economic justice taskforce why people of color were not attending meetings as faithfully as the Euro-American members of the committee. Instead of becoming defensive, the staff person had an "aha" moment and changed the practice of how dates were chosen for future meetings.

"In order to get a donkey to move, one must first get the donkey's attention." Another time when the Hispanics walked out of the General Synod one year because of institutional racism, it got the attention of the Synod delegates to move from merely "braying/praying" to taking concrete steps in the right direction.

Healing Racism

Racism is not a thing of the past that ended with the Civil Rights movement in the United States. It surrounds us every day. Not long ago, I was eyewitness to the assassination of a Samoan young man in public housing in Palolo who was killed because of his race. Perhaps in the next edition of this book, I will be able to tell that story in full, but witnessing that event has led to me experiencing Post-Traumatic Stress Disorder, so it's too difficult for me to tell it in full right now. That said, a similar story is depicted in the 2013 film *Fruitvale Station*, about the true story of the events leading up to the death of Oscar Grant, a young black man killed by a BART police officer at the Fruitvale Bay Area Rapid Transit (BART) Station in Oakland, California. We cannot close an eye to racism. The only solution is to understand and then heal it.

Racism is different from prejudice. The National Council of Churches defines racism as prejudice plus power. In other words, there is no such thing as reverse racism since minorities don't have power until they become a "majority" and can exercise power. In present day Hawai'i, Japanese-Americans and Euro-Americans have power.

Some of my friends will question my putting Japanese-Americans into the power equation in Hawai'i, and they are partly correct. In the listing of the Top 20 Richest People in Hawai'i, according to the 2012 issue of *Hawai'i Business* magazine, fifteen individuals were Euro-Americans, three Japanese-Americans, one Indian (from India), and one Chinese-American. Japanese-Americans may not have the same economic clout as their white counterparts, but they have much power in the education, legal, and political sectors.

One morning, my friends and I attended a court hearing for Marie Beltran and her family; they had refused to stop living on their Kanaka Maoli ancestral land at Mokuleia Beach, and as a result, faced fines and other court actions. You can learn more about Marie Beltran and her family's story in the video "Life on the Beach: A Visit with Marie Beltran" at http://www.youtube.com/watch?v=7Hs2Y_ZMc-s

During the break in the hearing, a friend pointed out a poster tacked on the wall of the courthouse showing judges and administrators of the Wahiawa court system. Out of about the about twelve people depicted with their last names beneath them, 100 percent were of Japanese-American background. The family was experiencing racism because its land was being illegally occupied by the U.S. and the court system full of Japanese-Americans tended to side with the occupation forces.

Dr. Keanu Sai, a Ph.D. graduate in political science from U.H. Manoa, teaches classes at the university level and to grassroots people. I challenge readers to visit www.HawaiianKingdom.org and listen to his two-hour lecture on why the present U.S. occupation of Hawai'i is illegal by international law. Let me know if you find any holes in his legal argument. The case is presently before the United Nations. It has already been argued at the World Court in the Netherlands.

Since racism is a virulent disease in Hawai'i, as is true elsewhere in the world, some of the churches have tried to address the need to "undo racism." Pacific Islander and Asian American Ministries (PAAM) of the United Church of Christ invited the Rev. C.T. Vivian, a colleague of Martin Luther King, Jr. and founder of BASICS (1), to lead three-day workshops on three occasions. C.T. Vivian was known to have provided the most effective training for undoing racism in many parts of the continental United States. I was privileged to attend a number of the trainings, both in Hawai'i and on the continent.

Because the training entailed people from dominant cultures "experiencing" racism in a very existential and emotionally wrenching way, a certain percentage of participants always left midway into the journey. But for those who stuck it out, metamorphosis took place. I prefer the word metamorphosis to "transformation" because one can be transformed one day and the next month relapse into one's former behavior. When a caterpillar enters its cocoon and emerges a butterfly, there is no way it can go back to being a caterpillar. That was the beauty of the C.T. Vivian experience. But after news spread about how real pain was experienced in these workshops, very few people in positions of power in our churches wanted to experience for themselves what it really felt like to be a person of color on the bottom rung of society with very little power—no wiggle room, so to speak.

More recently, those who have metamorphosed into an existential and deep understanding of racism have begun to unpack the evils of racism as "white privilege." Hopefully, headway is being made as Euro-Americans tackle the very difficult task of creating metamorphosis in their own communities.

Internalized racism, on the other hand, needs to be addressed by survivors who internalized the larger society's view of darker-skinned people as inferior. I am one of the survivors of this experience, having grown up in Hawai'i as part of the plantation milieu and with parents who could not speak English. To heal internalized racism, a person of color could participate in Undoing Internalized Racism workshops led in different parts of the country by various church and secular groups. The United Church of Christ, under the leadership of staff leader Juanita Helphrey, a member of the Hidatsa nation in the Dakotas, developed curriculum for dealing with internalized racism. Hopefully, the curriculum is still available under the auspices of Justice and Witness Ministries, UCC, in Cleveland, Ohio.

I encourage my readers also to read Frances E. Kendall's book *Understanding White Privilege*. More information can be found at: http://speakoutnow.org/downloads/Kendall.pdf

Nine to Five

While celebrating my birthday a few days ago—December 26, 2013—a close friend of my son made an interesting comment. She stated that I'd had the luxury of not having to work at a job all my life. I decided to take this statement as a compliment since my son Bob likes to brag that his mother never had to commute to a nine-to-five job. I think Bob was conveying that I was independent and resourceful and managed to work in situations where I was the boss. For the record, however, I needed to correct this misconception since I held many jobs where I had a boss looking over my shoulder. Still, Bob was partly correct because most of my nine-to-five jobs happened when he was a baby or a toddler.

The fact that Bob's friends thought I lived in "no boss" luxury world most of my life initiated all kinds of emotion on my birthday. I realized that I had not shared stories with Bob about the many jobs I held as a youth of fifteen and up until the present day. My purpose in writing this book is to share my stories with my son Bob, and hopefully, pass them on to my grandchildren in the years to come. In my way of thinking, sharing stories is "service to the community" because the more we "consult" with each other, the more truth and unity emerges.

Even before I was legally employable, I worked full-time in the summer of 1955 as the legal secretary to Attorney John Lanham, who was later elected to the Hawai'i State House of Representatives. I continued to work part-time with Mr. Lanham after school until I found another part-time job in 1957 at the Kapiolani Furniture and Appliance store in customer relations and as a cashier. Since the store was located one block from our home on Kuahiwi Street, it was a more convenient job location. In 1957, our family was still cooking on a kerosene stove and we did not have TV like most families in our neighborhood. One day, I came home with a TV in my arms and presented it to my mom and dad. I will never forget that day because Matsuo and Kyozo both cried out of joy and pride. They knew I had saved the money to purchase the television for the family—a luxury that they could not comprehend ever enjoying without the help of their children. Their tears made me realize the important economic role that children of immigrant families play in Hawai'i and throughout the world. Kyozo and Matsuo's great appreciation motivated me to continue working and saving all my life to make sure that my parents would not have the same worries that accompanied their earlier years as farmworkers. I also recalled that I was the tax preparer for my mom and dad as a sixth grader because they could not read and understand the IRS instructional book and forms, which were available only in English.

During my four years of study at the University of Hawai'i in Manoa, I also had many bosses since I worked part-time at the Economic Research Center in the basement of Hawaii Hall. Mr. Mark, the director of the Research Center, was a wonderful boss, and I still treasure photos of a Christmas party where five staff members passed oranges cheek-to-cheek and wrapped each other as mummies with toilet paper. Mr. Mark was a geek who knew how to be a fun boss.

As a graduate student at the School of Theology at Claremont, California, I worked in the school library as a part-time librarian and learned a lot about the Dewey Decimal System. Upon graduation from Claremont, I joined the staff of the First United Methodist Church in Oakland, California as the Director of Christian Education. My boss was Dr. Charles Lord, Senior Pastor of the church. Dr. Lord and his wife Velma treated me like one of their children, and those four years in East Oakland and Downtown Oakland were some of the happiest years of employment in my life. Since the church was an inner city church in two locations, I did a lot of knocking on doors. I never locked my car, so the police in the neighborhood would stuff my car full of newspapers to teach me a lesson...a lesson I refused to learn. Only once did I lose anything from my car in East Oakland. The early '60s in East Oakland was not troubled with drugs like the end of the decade. Because I worked with many of the black families in East Oakland, I was able to view the evolving history of the Black Panther movement in Oakland from the perspective of the black community. Huey Newton was a powerful speaker in large assemblies held regularly at the Oakland Auditorium, and I was able to attend some of those assemblies. Many of the churches in Oakland were cognizant of police violence against young black men, and sometimes, they offered their churches for breakfast programs and youth programs. The Downtown Oakland Christian Parish (DOCP) was formed during my tenure in Oakland and cooperative ministries for the urban core held much promise.

I want my son Bob to know that I also served as editor of the Berkeley Science Laboratory's newspaper in the mid-1970s. I had no experience as an editor, but I loved the challenge of editing *The Magnet*, a scientific newspaper written for laypersons. Many of these jobs were never listed in my Curriculum Vitae because they were often not related to the training I received at the Claremont School of Theology or the University of California at Berkeley. For the sake of brevity, I share the curriculum vitae I developed recently. (I don't believe in retirement.)

CURRICULUM VITAE

Julia Keiko Matsui Higa Estrella

Academic Training:

1952-1958: Leilehua High School, Wahiawa, Oahu, Hawai'i

1958-1962: Bachelor of Education, Univ. of Hawai'i, Manoa Campus

1962-1964: Master's of Education, Claremont School of Theology

1972-1974: Master's in Social Planning, University of California, Berkeley

Church Involvement:

1962-1964: Crusade Scholar, United Methodist Church

1972: Pacific Islander and Asian American Ministries (PAAM): Organizing Committee

1974: Delegate to the World Council of Churches Pre-Meeting, Tanzania

1975: Delegate to World Council of Churches, Nairobi, Kenya (One of eight delegates representing the United Church of Christ)

1975-1981: Executive Council, National United Church of Christ

1979: PAAM delegation to Japan and South Korea

1984-present: Council on Racial and Ethnic Ministries (COREM): Organizing Committee

1989: Delegate to Peace Conference, National Council of Churches, Moscow, USSR

1990: Delegate to Pacific Ecumenical Forum, Hilo, Hawai'i

1992: Delegate to Pacific Conference of Churches Convocation, Vanuatu

2005: Delegate to Peace for Life Ecumenical Consultation, Mindanao, Philippines

2007: PAAM delegation to American Samoa

Community Involvement:

1990-2005: USJCRJ's Tochi Wa Inochi (Land is Life): Okinawa, Guam, Vieques, Marshall Islands, Waianae-Oahu; Osaka-Japan Survivors and supporters of survivors (U.S./Japan militarism) met every 3-5 years in different locations listed above.

1995-2012: U.S. Japan Committee for Racial Justice (USJCRJ)

1996-2005: Supporter, Island Tenants on the Rise (ITOR)

1998-present: Supporter, Micronesians United, State of Hawai'i (MU)

2000-present: Supporter, ERUB (Enewetak, Rongelap, Utrik, Bikini) Survivors' Network

2006-2008: Hawai'i People's Fund, Honolulu, Hawai'i, Grants Committee

2009: Chair of Endowment Committee, National Pacific Islander and Asian American Ministries (PAAM)

Work Experience:

1964-1974: Director of Christian Education in Oakland, California; Sacramento, California; and El Cerrito, California in successive years

1973-1977: Administrative Assistant, City Councilwoman Ying Lee Kelley

1977-1978: City Planner, City of Las Vegas

1979-1980: Development Director, Community Economics, Inc., Oakland, California

1980-1990: Founder; 'Ohana Cultural Center, Oakland, California

1987-1995: Director of Pacific and Asian Center for Theologies and Strategies (PACTS) Berkeley, California

1996-present: Director of PACTS in Hawai'i (volunteer)

2010 to present: Adjunct Faculty, University of Hawai'i, Manoa Campus

Publications:

Contributing Writer: *The Cities Wealth* with Ed Kirshner, Lenny Goldberg, Eve Bach, et al. Washington, D.C.: Alternative State and Local Public Policies, 1976.

Contributing Writer: *Cry for Justice: The Churches and Synagogues Speak.* Robert McAfee Brown, editor. Paulist Press, 1991.

Contributing Writer: *Divestment from South Africa*, with Larry Litvak, Washington, D.C.: Alternative State and Local Public Policies, 1979.

Mother and Son

Bob feeds Leilani Murakami, the oldest daughter of Jeff Murakami.

Robert Estrella in Samoa

As a member of Pacific Islander and Asian American Ministries (PAAM), my son Robert was asked to video the solidarity visit of Hawai'i PAAM to Samoa from May 6-13, 2011.

The delegation included Ms. Haleaka Martin, Ronald Fujiyoshi, Ula Sao (a native of Samoa), and Robert. The delegation attended the weeklong meeting of the Elders of the Christian Congregational Churches of Samoa (CCCS) and their committee meetings.

The goals of the exposure/solidarity trip were accomplished in that the Elders of the CCCS welcomed the delegation, they were introduced during the Mission committee of the Elders, spoke during the Worship Service for Mission, and attended an annual meeting for the women of the CCCS. During the Mission committee of the Elders, the delegation was asked to explain Hawai'i-PAAM, national PAAM, and the United Church of Christ, and to answer questions from committee members. They shared their dream of cooperating with the CCCS and with Rev. Sala Nolan Gonzales, the Minister for Criminal Justice and Human Rights of the United Church of Christ, to work with the Samoan gangs in Hawai'i prisons. Their goals were met with positive reactions. The group also attended Sunday worship at Vaiala Church where Rev. Oka Fau'olo preached, attended the CCCS Christian Endeavor worship service led by Rev. Fuamaila Soa, Jr., and had a nine-

ty-minute audience with the Head of State Tui Atua Tupua
Tamasese Ta'isi Efi.

One of the highlights of their visit was to relax at the home of
Ula's parents and eat Sunday lunch with some of her brothers
and sisters who came to visit on Mother's Day. Everyone feast-
ed on octopus, eel, crab, *palusami*, fish, chicken, taro, bananas,
and a Samoan dessert made from papaya among other things.
Her brothers played the guitar and sang Samoan hymns as
they served their guests *kava* and the family enjoyed being
together. The PAAM members were impressed by how the
matai chieftain system in the villages, the pastors, churches,
and the Samoan culture still work together in a positive way
to bring harmony. The Head of State's leadership in trying to
live out the Samoan indigenous knowledge and restore it to
a central position in Samoan life is profound. PAAM and the
United Church of Christ have much to learn from Samoa and
the CCCS.

Following is some general information on Samoa:

Christianity is the dominant religion in Samoa. The major
languages spoken by the Samoa population are Samoan
and English. A major part of the population in Samoa is
engaged in agricultural production (64 percent). The rest
of the people in Samoa are in the service sector (30 percent). Samoans' religious adherence includes the following:
Christian Congregational Church of Samoa 35.5 percent,
Roman Catholic 19.6 percent, Methodist 15 percent, Latter-
Day Saints 12.7 percent, Samoan Assemblies of God 10.6
percent, Seventh-day Adventist 3.5 percent, Worship Centre
1.3 percent, unspecified 0.8 percent (2001 census).

The Head of State until 2007, His Highness Malietoa Tanumafili II, was a Baha'i convert. Samoa hosts one of seven Baha'i Houses of Worship in the world; completed in 1984 and dedicated by the Head of State, it is located in Tiapapata, 8 km (5 mi) from Apia.

Books written by O le Ao o le Malo (Head of State): Tui Atua Tupua Tamasese Ta'isi Efi are *Pacific Indigenous Dialogue on Faith, Peace, Reconciliation and Good Governance* and *Su'esu'e Manogi: In Search of Fragrance.*

Bob felt his trip to Samoa was important because he has many Samoan clients who use his videography service. By actually experiencing the homeland of his clients, he can share his experiences with them, and in turn, he receives many stories back, which brings him closer to the people, as "family" rather than "clients." You can view Robert's video of the delegation's visit to Samoa at: http://youtube/Ohar8jwPsIw

Part Three

THE FLOWERING TREE: SERVICE

"It is not man's reason
But the invisible Love of God
That generates the Power
To save humanity."

— Mokichi Okada

Signs of Hope: 'Ohana Ho'opakele

Officers of 'Ohana Ho'opakele.

As I reflect on the past year and look for Signs of Hope as we begin our New Year of 2014, the following events stand out for me:

- Movement for a living wage is gaining momentum in Hawai'i and nationally

- There is more awareness of the dangers of GMO (genetically modified) farming, leading to community action by consumers on the Big Island and on Kaua'i; the fever is spreading to other parts of Hawai'i as well

- Local, sustainable nature farming is on the rise and more families are shopping at farmers' markets throughout the state

- Although Borders Bookstore closed a few years ago, there is evidence that local small bookstores are beginning to thrive in communities where local authors are featured and supported

There are many more signs of hope in Hawai'i, but the biggest beacon of hope I see right now is the movement to set up a Pu'uhonua (refuge) on the Big Island of Hawai'i by a grassroots Kanaka Maoli (Native Hawaiian) group called 'Ohana Ho'opakele. 'Ohana Ho'opakele's vision points to a model Pu'uhonua where the traditional process of ho'oponopono (to make right) would be used along with other restorative justice methods to help repair the damages of crime for offender, victim, and all those affected by crime.

Kanaka Maoli residents of Hawai'i understand the reality that the criminal justice system's discriminatory treatment of Native Hawaiians is responsible for their disproportionate number in the criminal justice system—approximately 40-50 percent incarceration rate for a population of around 20 percent in Hawai'i. Their appeal for justice and call for support for a new way to "heal"—a prison without walls—is detailed below.

If the Pu'uhonua movement succeeds, it will have a major ripple effect on the continental U.S. as well.

The national press has given this movement a lot of media attention this past year because more and more states realize that traditional incarceration structures do not work and are too costly to maintain now and into the future.

Following is a letter from the president of this movement, Palikapu Dedman, with more information on its efforts:

'Ohana Ho'opakele (To Rescue the Family)

Please join us in establishing the first, modern *Pu'uhonua* or Wellness Center in Hawai'i to heal our *pa'ahao* (incarcerated) brothers and sisters!

Please help us show our *pa'ahao*, their families, the State of Hawai'i and the world our commitment to this model of healing!

'Ohana Ho'opakele badly needs some funding because:

- We hired Ms. Georgette Yaindl as our lawyer to challenge the Final Environmental Assessment on Kulani.

- We convinced 113 pa'ahao to join us in our lawsuit.

- We held a press conference on the steps of the Prince Kuhio Federal Building on November 8, 2013, inviting the Attorney General Eric Holder to come to Hawai'i and investigate why such a high number of Native Hawaiians are in prison.

- We are working with a businesswoman to develop our *P'uhonua* Plan, including curriculum and budget as the follow-up to Act 117

See more of what we are doing on our website at www.ohanahoopakele.org, or become our friend on our Facebook page, or email us at ohanahoopakele@gmail.com

To donate toward our effort, either write a check to 'Ohana Ho'opakele and mail it to P.O. Box 5530, Hilo, HI 96720, or scroll down the home page of our website and donate online by PayPal. ('Ohana Ho'opakele has received not-for-profit incorporation status by the State of Hawai'i and the U.S. government.)

Mahalo! (Thank you)

Palikapu Dedman, President

Oscar López Rivera

For a long time, I have been an admirer of Oscar López Rivera, who has been incarcerated for his efforts to bring about Puerto Rico's independence. Not only is he a symbol of independence for the people of Puerto Rico, but I believe he also stands as a symbol of hope for the people of Hawai'i.

Consequently, I was very honored and humbled to receive a handwritten letter from Oscar López Rivera, dated January 21, 2013. He wrote as follows:

Dear Julia:

Thank you for the birthday card and the letter.

It would be a great pleasure meeting you in Puerto Rico… I'm fairly certain I'll be there. When it will happen I have no idea. But I have plenty of hope.

During the past year the work around the campaign for my release has been very successful. In Puerto Rico the overwhelming majority of the people are supporting the demand for my release. Pres. Obama can't say the Puerto Rican people aren't supporting the campaign and that he is not aware of it.

I hope your trip to Haifa is all you want it to be. I can imagine how good the experiences are going to be. It's always pleasurable meeting different people, cultures and religions.

Have a joyous and safe trip.
Take good care, stay strong.
En Resistencia & Lucha,

Oscar López Rivera

I treasure this letter because Oscar López Rivera is such an inspiration to me and a symbol for the rights of people to be free and govern themselves.

Arrested in 1981 for his acts and beliefs in favor of the independence of Puerto Rico, Oscar López Rivera is the longest-held political prisoner in the history of Latin America. He was charged and convicted of seditious conspiracy—the same charge for which Nelson Mandela spent twenty-seven years in prison. Although he did not harm anyone, he was sentenced to seventy years in prison, ten times the average sentence for murder. In 1999, ten of his fellow-pro-independence prisoners were released; he was offered release in ten years, while two others were to remain behind bars. He declined the offer because he did not want to leave the two behind; both are now home and making positive contributions to civil society.

During his thirty-two years in prison, Rivera's granddaughter was born, played imaginary games with him through the glass that separated them when she was a preschooler, and has since graduated from high school and college.

Oscar's support includes religious and elected officials, performing artists, and organizations from across Puerto Rico's political and religious spectrum. Recognizing him as an inspiring leader whose wisdom and contributions are desperately needed by the family, society, and nation that await him, his fellow Puerto Ricans have united in the common struggle to bring him home.

Below, I am sharing with permission two of the thirteen letters he wrote to his granddaughter Karina in the hopes that our readers will visit the website listed below and read all thirteen letters. These letters will transform your life as they have mine. Mahalo.

1st Letter by Oscar López Rivera: "The Hands on the Prison Glass"

Dear Karina,

It hasn't been easy to choose a title for these letters that I am planning to send you periodically from prison.

Writing to you, whose childhood and adolescence I have already irretrievably lost, I feel that I am speaking to thousands of young Puerto Ricans, for whom my name means almost nothing.

I am a 70-year-old fighter. I have been imprisoned for 32 years. I will not elaborate on the political reasons that brought me to this confinement, because others have already done so. I only want to reiterate that above all else, I respect life, and that I have not hurt any human being, and never would.

The first time I saw you, in the summer of 1991, at the prison in Marion, Illinois, where I was held at the time, it was through a glass. You were in your mother's arms, and moved your eyes with curiosity. But there was little to see. The cubicle where the visits were held was very narrow, and there was a telephone on each side so that we could talk. Clarisa, your mother, lifted hers and asked me to say something to you. It was the first time that you heard my voice and I could see your reaction, the strangeness that it caused you to communicate with this man who had begun to love you, but who could not kiss you, nor whisper in your ear the grandfather's promises that he wanted to make to you.

They let Clarisa bring in three diapers and some bottles of milk in her bag. In the visiting area, both on the family's side and on the prisoners', there were cameras that recorded all of our movements, but, ironically, I could never take a photo of my daughter and granddaughter. Three or four guards always escorted me, and I was chained by my feet. I was the only prisoner who was guarded so heavily in the visitors' area.

It was difficult to entertain you while you were in the visiting cubicle, so to distract you and help your mother, who was trying to spend the longest possible time with me, we invented a peculiar game: you would put your small infant hands on the glass, and I would also put mine on it, so that the four would coincide and we could "touch." The hands would jump, and chase each other, and behave like spiders wrapped in the invisible threads of love. We could not touch—the glass prevented us—but a special language emerged between you and me—between your tender hands, Karina, and my old ones, pale from confinement, wanting to be able to fly, but contented and humbled when you caressed them.

Throughout the years we used that dance of the hands to communicate with each other. Time passed and you grew up. I wasn't permitted physical contact with my family, so that during the years that I was held in Marion, I couldn't kiss you, hug you, or feel the touch or scent of your hair. Nor of your mother, who bade me farewell with tears, although I knew how to contain my own.

One day, finally, they transferred me to the prison in Terre Haute, Indiana. There they told me that I could receive visits and have physical contact with my loved ones. Your mother arrived with you and my niece Wanda. You, Karina, were only seven. My daughter and niece embraced me. But you stood in front of me, raised your hands, and stuck them on an imaginary glass, waiting for me to do the same. At your tender age, after so many years of enduring this barrier, you thought that we should continue the game. Your mother told you: "Now you can touch your grandfather," and you ran to embrace me, and we touched for the first time.

That glass, despite everything, continues being our accomplice. Through it, on these pages, I will continue relating my memories and current stories, to you, my longed-for granddaughter.

With much, much love, in resistance and struggle….

Oscar López Rivera

2nd Letter by Oscar López Rivera: "Where the Sea Breathes"

This is the second letter of Rivera to his granddaughter Karina Published Sept 14, 2013

Oscar López Rivera / imprisoned for 32 YEARS

On Saturday, the Puerto Rican newspaper *El Nuevo Día* periodically publishes letters that political prisoner Oscar López Rivera sends from jail to his granddaughter Karina, who has only known him through the prison bars.

Dear Karina,

After the family, what I miss most is the sea.

Thirty-five years have passed since the last time I saw it. But I have painted it many times, the Atlantic part as well as the Caribbean, that smiling foam of light mixed with salt in Cabo Rojo.

For any Puerto Rican, it is almost incomprehensible to live far from the sea. It's one thing when you know that you are free to move wherever you want and travel to see it. It doesn't matter if it's cold and gray. Even if you're seeing it from a distant shore, you realize that it is always beginning again (as a poet said), and that through this sea, the fish that had been near your land can come to you, bringing memories of home.

I learned to swim at a young age; I must've been about three years old. A cousin of my father, who lived with us and was like an older brother to me, used to take me to the beach where he swam with his friends, and throw me into the water so that I would learn. Later, when I was in school, I would escape to a nearby river with other kids. Now this all seems very far away.

Here in prison I have often felt nostalgia for the sea; to fill my lungs with its scent; to touch it and wet my lips—but instantly I realize that it may be many years before I enjoy this simple pleasure.

I always missed the sea, but I think that I never needed it more than when they transferred me from the prison in Marion, Illinois, to the one in Florence, Colorado. In Marion, I went to the patio once a week, and from there I saw the trees, the birds…. I would hear the noise of the train and the song of the cicadas. I ran on the earth and smelled its fragrance. I could pick the grass and let the butterflies surround me. But in Florence, all that came to an end.

Do you know that the ADX, which is the maximum security prison in Florence, is the destination of the worst criminals in the U.S. and is considered the hardest and most impregnable of the country? There the prisoners have no contact among themselves; it is a labyrinth of steel and cement constructed to isolate and incapacitate. I was part of the first group of prisoners to be held there. When I got there, they woke me up various times throughout the night and for much of the time I did not manage to sleep for more than 50 minutes at a time. In that galley there were only four of us, but one of them had a long history of mental problems and he spent the night shouting obscenities, fighting his battle against invisible enemies. We were in our cells almost all the time, and even ate in them. All the furniture was made of reinforced concrete and could not be moved. I could not understand how the people in the town of Florence had accepted having such an inhuman prison in their neighborhood. But, day by day, the prison industry is among the strongest in the U.S. It produces money and that seems to be the only thing that matters to them.

In Florence, at night, the prisoners would communicate through a sort of vent near the ceiling. We had to shout in order to be heard; everyone shouted and that got on our nerves.

I kept quiet and tried to concentrate on the sound of the waves, closed my eyes and I saw them break on the Indian Cave. The cacophony of the prison went on fading. The sea rose and fell like someone's chest, contagious with its living force.

I know that one day I will spend all night on the coast, and I will wait until the break of day. Later I would like to do the same in Jayuya, to see the sun disappear over the cordillera.

With this hope, in resistance and struggle, your grandfather embraces you...

To read all thirteen letters, visit www.boricuahumanrights.org.

My interest in Puerto Rico's independence began when I met Alejandro Molina (a Mexican American activist who has devoted most of his life for the self-determination of Puerto Ricans in the United States). I met Alejandro in San Francisco when he was working closely with Dr. Kekuni Blaisdell to organize the Peoples' International Tribunal, Hawai'i 1993. The Tribunal invited judges and lawyers from all over the world to sit on a panel and hear the stories from grassroots Kanaka Maoli regarding the abridgement of their human rights as a result of the occupation of Hawai'i by the United States. I attended the two-week Tribunal in August 1993, which moved from island to island to hear the testimonies of the people. The stories of the people were very moving and brought tears to most of us in the audience on a daily basis. Additional testimonies from The Tribunal are available on a CD/DVD produced by Na Maka o ka'Aina by e-mailing namaka@interpac. net. One can also visit the website to see a whole host of tapes available on Hawaiian history, culture, language, movement activities, and so on at www.namaka.com.

According to the United Nations (General Assembly Resolution 1514) "All peoples have the right to self-determination; by virtue of that right they freely determine their political status."

This resolution of the United Nations undergirds the movement to free Oscar Lopez Rivera. Oscar did not kill anyone; he is a charismatic leader of the Puerto Rican people who see independence for Puerto Rico. His charge is "sedition," the same charge under which Nelson Mandela was sent to prison. Even the people who seek statehood or a commonwealth acknowledge the important role Oscar is playing for the common good of his people. Thus when he is released, it is expected that there will be an outpouring of people into the streets of Puerto Rico in celebration and in jubilation by all sectors of society for their national hero. I plan to be there.

Letter from Nozomi Ikuta

I met Nozomi Ikuta through the PAAM movement in 1978.

January 7, 2014

Dear Julia,

It is interesting to reflect on the ways our lives have intersected and intertwined regarding Oscar and the other, now-released political prisoners, and the United Church of Christ (UCC).

Personally, I first became aware of many of them in the mid-1980s, while serving as a Commissioner for the Commission for Racial Justice (CRJ), the unit in the national United Church of Christ that existed until 2000 to promote racial justice. Alejandrina Torres, one of the prisoners and wife of the late Rev. José A. Torres, had been brutally assaulted in prison and the CRJ staff had asked us, its board, to approve a resolution of support for her and her family. Then, in 1987, when I was running for Secretary of the UCC—a story for another day, which you know about; I had been drafted by people of color to run as a protest)—the late Irma Romero came up to me and asked if I would support the political prisoners if I won and became Secretary. Honestly, I had no idea what "supporting" them really meant, but I said yes to Irma. (Not too many people to my knowledge ever said "no" to Irma.) Thank goodness I lost—I had no idea what supporting them might have entailed, and what I really wanted to do at that time in my life was have another baby. (Our second child, now twenty-five, was conceived a few months later.)

In the summer of 1991, the General Synod of the UCC adopted a resolution supporting the release of the Puerto Rican political prisoners. I had nothing to do with the writing or passage of that resolution, but it formed part of the policy base for my new job at the United Church Board for Homeland Ministries, part of the old national UCC structure, which I began at their then new offices in Cleveland a few weeks later. (That office was previously held by Rev. Alfonso Román, who paved the way for much of the work that was to follow.) That same resolution directed the President of the UCC to visit the Puerto Rican political prisoners, which Rev. Paul Sherry fulfilled during his first year in office by visiting Alejandrina Torres at the prison in Dublin, in northern California. Several other Puerto Rican political prisoners were held at the same prison—Dylcia Pagán, Lucy Rodriguez, and Carmen Valentín, along with several white political prisoners (Marilyn Buck, Linda Evans, and Laura Whitehorn).

During that time, you were living in Berkeley and were already visiting the political prisoners, and pretty soon, you were encouraging me to do the same. Once I did, there was no turning back—as you know, visiting them is a knock-your-socks-off experience after which it is very difficult to return to business as usual. You were also the one who introduced me to Alejandro Molina, one of the main leaders in the campaign to free these prisoners, who gave me concrete suggestions for ways to contribute to this work.

In 1995, the General Synod was held at your back door— in Oakland, California. People in the Bay Area organized a demonstration in support of the release of the Puerto Rican political prisoners, and delegates and visitors from the Synod took part in it. In the meantime, a delegation comprised of the Rev. Dr. Paul Sherry, President of the UCC, Rev. Dr. Thomas Dipko, Executive Vice President (effectively, the CEO) of the United Church Board for Homeland Ministries, and Rev. Linda Jaramillo, then President of the Council for Hispanic Ministries, visited the women at Dublin and returned to hold a press conference in which they spoke powerfully about how deeply moved they were by their visit. Ms. Jaramillo (she was ordained a few years after the visit) recounted a story Carmen told, about how her granddaughter Karina, who is also Oscar's granddaughter, had never been able to visit Oscar except through the glass of the prison visiting cubicle in Marion (very different from the relatively comfortable visiting room at Dublin) during her five years of life. Ms. Jaramillo related Carmen's description of the imaginary game that Karina played with Oscar through the glass, matching their hands up and pretending that they could touch each other.

The UCC and many other denominations, especially in Puerto Rico, rallied around the fifteen prisoners, including a massive march of 100,000 people in San Juan in

August of 1999. A few weeks later, eleven of the prisoners came home.

The years passed. I changed jobs within the UCC in 2000 and left in 2003; Rev. Sala Nolan Gonzales continued the work I had done through the UCC and visited Oscar in the mid-2000s.

Antonio Camacho Negrón had already completed his sentence; Juan Segarra Palmer was released in 2004, and Carlos Alberto Torres, who was not included in President Clinton's offer, was released on parole in July, 2010. Of all the Puerto Rican political prisoners arrested in the 1980s, Oscar alone remains in prison.

In 2011, the General Synod renewed its commitment to Oscar. In 2012, Revs. Geoffrey Black, President of the UCC, and Linda Jaramillo, now Executive Minister of Justice and Witness Ministries, visited him with Rev. Nolan. In September, *El Nuevo Día,* a newspaper in Puerto Rico, began publishing his letters to his granddaughter, Karina, now a graduate of the University of Chicago. The series, called "Hands on the Glass," begins with Oscar's re-counting of his game with Karina on the prison glass—the same game that Carmen had related to us through Rev. Jaramillo nearly twenty years ago.

During the time of your involvement with this issue, Julia, our relationships with the UCC have changed; Rev. Torres and Irma Romero have passed; Karina has grown from infant to adult, and the women you used to visit in California have been out of jail and contributing to their families and the broader society for over fourteen years.

The UCC has been a consistent thread in the tapestry of support for these prisoners over the years, as manifest in the interweaving of our narrative with the topics in Oscar's letters. That thread **would have existed** even without you, but it would be missing many strands and stitches. Thanks very much for all you have done to weave the fabric of justice and love.

Mahalo to you for your love of *pono* (righteousness) and steadfast commitment to truth and freedom.

In a follow-up letter on January 9, 2014, Nozomi sent me this additional information:

The prisoners were released on September 10, 1999.

At first, the Puerto Rican women at Dublin were Dylcia Pagán, Ida Luz Rodríguez (Lucy), Alejandrina Torres, and Carmen Valentín. Later, Alejandrina was transferred to Danbury, CT and Alicia Rodríguez came from the state prison to Dublin.

In light of our conversation, I'm going to insert a couple of additional sentences, as this writing connects much more with you and your role than the other piece that I did. Basically, the other piece was very dry and academic—I had intended to write something a bit fuller but didn't have time until yesterday. It's up to you what you do with it, but writing helped me see your role in all of this more clearly.

The truth is that if you had not introduced me to Alejandro, I might not have gotten as involved as I did. Your work at New Fellowship was very important, but your outreach to me helped catalyze the involvement of the UCC executive types, and through them, the ecumenical support.

Thanks very much for your work and legacy!

Nozomi Ikuta

Lead On, O Cloud of Yahweh

I can't remember when and where I first sang the hymn "Lead On, O Cloud of Yahweh," but it became my favorite hymn because of the concept that one is on a lifelong spiritual journey and we follow the Cloud of Yahweh wherever the cloud leads us. The spiritual journey is indeed our "home."

When my father came to Hawai'i to work on the sugar plantations, his spirituality was based in the Buddhist religion because it was part of the culture he grew up in. My mother came from Okinawa with her indigenous spirituality where Mother Nature was central because it was a part of her culture.

Both of my parents converted to Christianity when missionaries from Japan came to Hawai'i through the Oriental Missionary Japanese Holiness Church. The church they attended was called "King's Chapel" and was located on Westervelt Street in Wahiawa. As a toddler, I remember "belting out" hymns in Japanese and smiling faces would turn in my direction. It was good to be noticed and affirmed. Because the church was located one block from our home, many members would walk over to our home for a fellowship lunch. It was there in the midst of this Japanese-speaking church that I learned the beauty of "spiritual and food fellowship."

I also learned that I had to be bi-cultural in the context of Hawai'i. In Japanese culture, I was taught that I could not accept a gift unless I said "No" three times. If the person offering the gift insisted three times, then I could accept the gift. However, I learned quickly that when non-Japanese people offered gifts, if I said, "No," they would withdraw their offers immediately. Since most of the offerings were sought-after candies, my sister Ruth and I quickly learned the rules of the game. We said "Yes" immediately when Euro-Americans offered candy and "No" three times followed by a "Yes" when Japanese church members offered sweets. It was in the context of church meetings and fellowship at our home that I learned Japanese culture. The culture was not taught by words but by action. We children observed and learned the rules of the culture.

Since the Holiness denomination was conservative in theology, it did not tolerate any bending of the church teachings, especially of the Ten Commandments. Therefore, when Rev. Shimatori, the pastor of King's Chapel, divorced his wife and remarried, the church went in many directions. Our family, along with a significant group of King's Chapel members, ended up attending another church in the neighborhood— the Wahiawa Methodist Church. The members of this church were mostly white and the congregation accommodated this influx of Japanese-speaking people by allowing a Japanese-speaking congregation to exist side-by-side with the English-speaking congregation. I was five at that time, and since I was learning English in kindergarten, it was a good laboratory to practice both my English, my Japanese, and my pidgin (with the Sunday school class, made up mostly of local children.)

I loved Sunday school because of the hymn singing; therefore, I never missed a Sunday. The Sunday school gave out pins and awards every year for perfect attendance, and I was the only one who received them eight years in a row. However, when I turned thirteen, I began asking a lot of questions in Sunday school. I remember very clearly raising my hand and asking, "If my ancestors in Japan and Okinawa never heard of Jesus, would they be in hell and not in heaven?" And the teacher said, "Yes." I think that is when I began to question the Christian faith—the "only" way to heaven being through Jesus became a sticking point with me.

However, I still attended church regularly because I wanted to please my parents, plus the youth programs provided great leadership training opportunities. We also met other young people from all over the island through square-dancing events with Mr. McGiffen, the caller. Each church youth group from different parts of the island would attend square-dancing in a uniform skirt. Our Wahiawa youth group wore yellow and white plaid skirts. Tears come to my eyes just remembering what happy times we had at those fun nights. All through junior high and high school, my sister and I also attended one-week summer camps at Camp Kailani, located right on the beach in Kailua. These were heavenly adventures and the best part of our teen years.

The Methodist Church paid for 100 percent of my education at the University of Hawai'i in Manoa, and 100 percent of my graduate studies at Claremont School of Theology in southern California. The denomination's membership at that time was close to ten million members, and the national church made a great investment in youth by providing scholarships globally. I was part of a Crusade scholarship program where nearly 200 students from all over the world met in Washington, D.C. for two weeks to be oriented to American culture and then were sent out all over the U.S. to pursue our theological studies. In 1962, Hawai'i was considered to be a mission outpost connected to the Southern California conference. At first, the national church did not want to grant scholarships to those from Hawai'i (since we had become a state of the United States in 1959). However, the leadership in Hawai'i argued that Hawai'i was considered a "mission" territory as far as the denomination was concerned. Thus three of us from Hawai'i became the first students to be considered part of the Crusade program.

The Cloud of Yahweh led me to the Congregational Church when a Methodist pastor who was serving as an interim pastor at Sycamore Congregational Church invited me to be part of the staff as the Director of Christian Education. My poem in Part 2 of this book titled "Mary and Miya" tells of my first meeting with Mary Tomita, who came knocking at my door with the invitation from Sycamore Church. Many wonderful years were spent in the company of Sycamore members. If one googles "Shochiku Bai," a story written by Clifford Alika and Miya Okawara, one will get the wonderful flavor of the Japanese-American congregational movement in California, Seattle, and Chicago.

Because a Methodist pastor invited me to Sycamore, I would often joke that I was sent as a missionary to the Congregational Church. Therefore, from the day Mary Tomita knocked at our student dorm until just recently (a span of about forty-two years), I was active in the congregational system and attended the General Synod in 1973, when the Congregationalists united with another denomination and became the United Church of Christ. I felt at home with the United Church of Christ because it was a Peace and Justice denomination with a belief in the inclusivity of all peoples. I became active in the interfaith movement when I became Director of the Pacific and Asian American Center for Theologies and Strategies (PACTS), located at the Graduate Theological Union in Berkeley, California, in 1987. PACTS started out as part of the ecumenical movement in the Bay area, but early on, I became part of the interfaith movement nationally. Serving PACTS and the wider community for nine years before moving back to Hawai'i because of my husband's health was the happiest years of ministry for me. At age thirteen, I was already an interfaith believer, so my passion for affirming all religions seemed second nature to me.

About three years ago, I was invited to sit on the National Governance Committee of the United Church of Christ— the Committee's task was to restructure the denomination for present realities. Most mainline denominations are suffering from a decline in membership and income and most are going through restructuring programs as well. Our Pacific Islander and Asian American group known as PAAM took a position within the denomination that moving toward a "corporate" model with a hierarchical structure that meant less grassroots involvement was not the way to go. In the process of sitting on the Governance Committee, I saw the "divide and conquer" method used by powerful leaders within the denomination, especially trying to divide the unity within all of our racial and ethnic communities.

Needless to say, I was disheartened by the "behind closed doors"—nontransparent activities—that I saw happening all around me.

The Cloud of Yahweh beckoned to a movement right in my own backyard. I was a volunteer with Micronesians United, a group working for the rights of the newest immigrant group in Hawai'i. My personal experience growing up with non-English speaking parents showed me the difficulties being faced by Micronesians who migrated to Hawai'i. One of the main reasons for the large outmigration from Micronesia to Hawai'i was that the United States exploded sixty-seven bombs in the Marshall Islands with the nuclear radiation reaching out to all of Micronesia. When one's homeland (including the ocean) is poisoned and becomes a wasteland and one's people are used as a human experimental project (Project 4.1), it is no wonder that so many people come from all regions of Micronesia, seeking appropriate health care, better education for their children, and jobs to support their families in Hawai'i as well as support their families back home in Micronesia.

In the midst of their struggles, the Baha'i Faith in Hawai'i was reaching out to the homeless in Waianae and to the Micronesians in public housing. Since I was already working with Micronesians United and also working with the homeless in Hawai'i, it was natural to team up with a spiritually-based group whose focus was the same.

I thought the Baha'i group was a cult until Sisan Suda showed me a picture of the Shrines of the Bab and Abdul'baha and the Baha'i Gardens located in Haifa, Israel. This place looked like one of the Wonders of the World, perhaps the ninth Wonder of the World. So I began attending devotionals and firesides, asked many questions, and did an independent investigation of the faith.

Being an interfaith person for most of my life, it felt like the Cloud of Yahweh had led me to a home in my spiritual journey where Baha'i beliefs coincided with mine. Since I did not believe in a hierarchical and a corporate top-down leadership structure, I felt naturally at home. And although I had graduated from a Christian seminary, I did not believe in becoming ordained or "set apart" from the rest of the congregation. Priests and pastors had been needed in the days when they were the only ones who were educated to read the holy texts, but in this day and age of universal education, anyone can read any holy text and become spiritually uplifted.

In brief, the Baha'i teachings emphasize the following:

- There is only one God
- All major religions come from God
- All humanity is one family
- Women and men are equal
- The family and its unity are very important
- Everyone must receive an education
- All prejudice, whether it is racial, religious, national, or economic, is destructive
- World Peace, upheld by a world government, is the crying need of our time
- Religion must be in harmony with science
- We must investigate truth for ourselves, without preconceptions
- An international auxiliary language will promote understanding among peoples

- Economic and environmental problems can be solved by the application of spiritual principles
- Confidence in an afterlife promotes nobility and continuing personal growth
- God's creation is essentially good, and we are all meant to be happy

I also want to clarify that I see the Baha'i faith as a continuation of my belief in Jesus. Baha'is believe in Jesus as one of the Christs who came to teach us the WAY. Baha'is believe in "progressive" revelation so Baha'u'llah is the most recent revelation…this happens about every 1,000 years or so (if one checks the progression from Buddha to Moses to Jesus to Mohammed, etc.)

Finally, another belief that Baha'is have that attracts me is their emphasis on interfaith beliefs and in solidarity. These beliefs tie in with my interests in social justice and how we must come together and work together to accomplish anything successfully. Solidarity has the ability to move mountains, as evidenced by people like Gandhi in India and Aung San Suu Kyi of Myanmar, who led a peaceful movement for change in her country. She was under house arrest under a harsh military dictatorship for many, many years. Now she is in Parliament and thinking about running for president. When people come together, they can accomplish amazing things.

Last February, my son and I journeyed to the Holy Land to visit Jerusalem and the Baha'i Holy Lands. My son was not a Baha'i when he accompanied me first to Istanbul and then to Adrianople, both in Turkey. But he had finished Book One in the Baha'i core studies program and also Book Four in the series while traveling in Istanbul. We arrived in Haifa the third week in February and proceeded to the Guest Center, where the official pilgrimage was to start at 2 p.m. People were milling around enjoying tea and snacks, so Bob and I joined one of the tables. Sitting at this table was a family of five—mother, father, and three teenagers. As we were getting acquainted, I mentioned that my son Bob was not a Baha'i but was rather on this pilgrimage to carry my suitcases. The mother, Mrs. Yguaran, who was sitting next to Bob, quickly turned around, looked him in the eye, and said, "I invite you to become Baha'i." That was the only invitation he needed. Bob said, "Yes," because he had been reading the Baha'i core studies program and felt he was ready to make the commitment. Now he was a Baha'i even before the official pilgrimage began. Thus began a most memorable pilgrimage—one that Bob and I will forever cherish. The Yguaran family took us in and fed us many a night—our hotel rooms were across the street from each other. This family became such an important part of our life that I have included a color photo of our 'ohana. We continue to be in touch with each other through Facebook and we look forward to the day when they will visit us in Hawai'i.

I was introduced to the Baha'i faith by Chris Cholas. Chris joined our Micronesians United group on Oahu and became a strong supporter. In the process of working together, Chris would often bring me to the National Baha'i Center near my friend Kekuni Blaisdell's home. He was eager to introduce me to members of their National Assembly and their counselor, who was from New Zealand. I noticed that Baha'is had a global vision and sent people out all over the world as volunteers. These committed individuals found work to support themselves wherever they went, and they worked side-by-side with the people, and their attitude was always a desire to learn from the people.

The *Encyclopedia Britannica* writes that Baha'is are the second most globally present religious body. In other words, wherever you go in the world, you will always find Baha'is present—at least a core group working in the community side-by-side with the people. When my son and I participated in the ten-day pilgrimage in Haifa a year ago, we found 200 people from all over the world—Haiti, Guyana, Venezuela, Colombia, Finland, Belgium, the Netherlands, the Philippines, Japan, Indonesia, Africa, India, China, and so on. Every two weeks throughout the year, the Haifa Pilgrim Center receives groups of approximately 200 people per session—an amazing range of people from all corners of the world. Now I have a more global vision and hope one day perhaps to become a volunteer in Africa, India, or Asia.

I once applied to the United Church of Christ to be a short-term missionary to the Philippines; I received so much paper-work to fill out and was told I had to get all the vaccinations necessary to become a missionary. When I asked the local Baha'i what I needed to do to volunteer with them in the Philippines or wherever the need was greatest, I was told that all I had to do was to alert the Pioneer desk locally so it could alert the Pioneer desk on the receiving end. And I would have to pay for all my expenses and support myself wherever I went. Someday I hope I might be able to do pioneering work in some part of the globe—perhaps Finland, Thailand,

Vietnam, Prince Edward Island—places that seem to beckon to me for some reason.

I also discovered that Baha'is in Hawai'i are considered part of the Pacific and not part of North America. The United States Baha'is have their own National Assembly and Hawai'i has its own independent National Assembly. I think Baha'u'llah and 'Abdu'l-baha had the correct vision of the future of Hawai'i as a sovereign nation interacting with national assemblies in the Pacific.

Apology Bill

PUBLIC LAW 103-150

To acknowledge the 100th annniversary of the Jan. 17, 1893, overthrow of the Kingdom of Hawai'i, and to offer an apology to Native Hawaiians on behalf of the United States for the overthrow of the Kingdom of Hawai'i.

Signed by President William Clinton on Nov. 23, 1993

Baha'i Gardens in Haifa, Israel

Shrine of the Bab and Shrine of Abdul'baha.

Yuri Kochiyama

Yuri Kochiyama, front row, far right.

One of my friends who always inspires me with her advocacy for social justice is Yuri Kochiyama.

Forty-nine years ago—on February 21, 1965—Malcolm X was gunned down in the Audubon Ballroom in Harlem. Yuri Kochiyama cradled his head as he lay dying on the stage. Malcolm was thirty-nine years old. An article in *Life* magazine immediately following the assassination shows Yuri cradling Malcolm's head.

For over sixty years, Yuri Kochiyama has championed civil rights, protested racial inequality, and fought for social justice causes. Her story begins during World War II. On the day of the bombing of Pearl Harbor, Yuri's father was arrested because he was a leader in the community. Sadly, it was also true that in some cases, Christians (who were more assimilated) turned in Buddhists (who tended to be more traditional in their Japanese ways or who had more contact with people in Japan). Her parents were then forcibly removed from their home by the U.S. government and held in an internment camp along with 120,000 other Japanese-Americans. While at a camp in Arkansas, Yuri came face-to-face with the segregation of the Jim Crow South. She immediately saw the parallels between the oppression of black people and the treatment of Japanese-Americans. In 1960, Yuri and her husband Bill Kochiyama moved into a public housing project in Harlem. Yuri became involved in the Civil Rights Movement and was part of the major struggles of the 1960s and '70s. She especially supported the black liberation struggle. In 1977, she took part in the takeover of the Statue of Liberty to bring attention to the struggle for Puerto Rican independence.

Whenever I visited New York City in the 1980s and '90s, I always knew I had a place to stay. When Yuri would take me on evening strolls in Harlem, she would be greeted warmly by so many of her friends and neighbors, who were also on an evening stroll to "talk story." Today, Yuri is part of an Asian women's group in the Bay area of which I am a member. I visited with Yuri about six months ago at a convalescent home in Berkeley. Yuri continues to be a mentor and inspiration to so many people, young and old, because of her undaunting spirit and desire to work for "fairness" in every aspect of life and for all communities.

By googling Yuri's name on the Internet, you can find more about her, including a long article about her life in the *New York Times*, plus many articles and videos highlighting her work throughout the years. I encourage you to read her memoir, *Passing It On*.

Peace for Life

I represented the Pacific and Asian American Center for Theologies and Strategies (PACTS) at the First People's Forum on Peace for Life in Davao, Mindanao, Philippines from Nov. 28 to December 4, 2004. My family and friends were worried that U.S. delegates, including myself, would be kidnapped because of all the stereotypes that exist about the Muslim resistance movement in Mindanao. I found Davao City to be a special place of beauty, cleanliness, and hospitality.

Originally conceived as a mainly-Christian ecumenical initiative in solidarity with other faith groups, "Peace for Life" was affirmed in Davao City as a place for people whose varied spiritualities—regardless of creed—are nurtured as a collective resource for resistance to all forms of injustice. The forum recognized the urgency of such coming together in the face of the flagrant misuse of religion for profit.

Carmencita Karagdag, the organizer and main spokesperson for Peace for Life over the last ten years, has been a special friend of mine since our first meeting at the World Council of Churches gathering in Nairobi, Kenya, in 1975. She was serving as a youth steward at this consultation. I was surprised one night when Carmencita and several other young stewards from the Philippines cornered me and asked whether I could get on the stage of the World Council and denounce the action of President Marcos, who had just announced martial law in the Philippines. I was very hesitant, and I knew that speakers could not go on stage without going through many hurdles. But to my shock and total amazement, these young people somehow managed to maneuver the heavily-guarded agenda of the World Council and were soon pushing me on to the stage. Standing before thousands, I was without words for a few moments. Since my husband was a professor at the University of the Philippines (on leave for studies at U.C. Berkeley), I spoke about my ties to the Philippines. I think my strongest point, however, was to indicate that I was a U.S. taxpayer and I opposed the use of my tax monies to prop up a dictator in the Philippines.

Ever since that moment, Carmencita and I have been supporting each other's justice and peace work. I attended subsequent Peace for Life consultations in New York and was hoping to join the one in South Korea held in November of 2013, but meeting my book deadline had to take precedence over making the trip. Peace for Life has accomplished many worthy goals in the ten years of its existence. I invite you to visit www.peaceforlife.org to learn more and to become a supporter of this very important spiritual and action-oriented movement.

Lessons from Civil Disobedience Actions

I worked as an intern at the office of Ying Lee Kelley while attending graduate school at UC-Berkeley. Ying was the first Asian American elected to the Berkeley City Council, and I felt very fortunate to be working with her—a great boss!

One day, Ying invited me to join her at a demonstration at University Hall, where students were calling the Trustees of the entire UC campus system to divest their funds from South Africa, as requested by Mandela's group.

At the demonstration, there was a call to block the entrances to University Hall. Around forty people stepped up to participate in a civil disobedience action. Suddenly, Councilwoman Ying Lee gently pushed me forward and said, "You and I need to get arrested…look, only blacks and whites are stepping forward…we need to show that Asians are in solidarity too." So we were arrested, fingerprinted, and released on location. A month later, I received a letter indicating that all charges were dropped.

Lesson learned: When you participate with a large group, charges will usually be dropped, if the demonstrators are nonviolent.

The second time, I was a bit more prepared to participate in a civil disobedience action. I happened to be on the island of

Kaua'i when there was a call from the Native Hawaiian community to participate in a religious procession to the Pacific Missile Range Facility (PMRF), where a missile was scheduled for the following day. The missiles were being launched from Kaua'i to the Marshall Islands, where the U.S. missile would intercept a "dummy" missile being launched from the U.S./ Marshall Islands military facility. Since some of my friends were participating, I joined in this peaceful march.

The fence at PMRF was a strange phenomenon—there was a gated fence with openings at both ends. The organizers of the march indicated that we would ask to go on the military base to hold a service for the Kanaka Maoli (Native Hawaiians) who were buried on the dunes of the beach. Rev. Kaleo Patterson was to be the main negotiator. If the negotiations did not go well, Rev. Patterson would motion our group to start walking into the military base from both ends of the gate.

After two hours of failed negotiations, Rev. Patterson motioned to our group to move in. Approximately twelve of us started to walk into the base, while the majority remained back to make sure that the news went out to the larger community and also to serve as "support." Suddenly, soldiers in uniform jumped out of the bushes and started to tackle the men in the group. The women were just handcuffed.

A video I have of this action clearly shows there is racism even in how people are arrested. The Kanaka Maoli in the group were tackled very roughly and shackled around their wrists until it hurt, while Asian Americans were not tackled, and a tall blonde female pastor was not even touched. She looked around befuddled for a long time while the rest of us were being arrested, and she finally walked out because the soldiers were refusing to arrest her.

Once we were handcuffed, we were put on a military bus. An officer came into the bus and said that we would all be asked to get off the bus one at a time in order to be interrogated. We all responded in one voice, "No, we are not getting off the bus." The military is not used to hearing "NO," only "YES, SIR." The officer was so discombobulated that he immediately got off the bus to report back to his superiors.

About half an hour later, another military officer got on the bus and announced that we were going to be turned over to the civil authorities in Lihue, an hour's ride away. Around twelve soldiers boarded the bus and stood up in the center aisle of the bus watching over us. During the hour-long ride, we all sang and told jokes and laughed a lot. I think the twelve soldiers were mystified that we were having a party on the bus and were not submissive to the authorities around us.

Once we reached Lihue, civilian police officers called us into their offices and asked for our particulars. We had no identification on us and the organizers told us that we were all either John Doe or Jane Doe. Therefore, while we were being questioned, we answered that we were seven feet tall, and weighed 200 pounds, or whatever good humor responses seemed appropriate. The civilian police took out their ticket books, jotted down our answers, and then released us with citations that were meaningless since our real names and addresses were not on the tickets. I now wish I had kept my citation in order to frame it for my friends to see. Unfortunately, I was not very memorabilia-conscious in those days.

Lesson Learned: The demonstration was successful in postponing the launching of the missiles to the Marshall Islands for several days, which was costly to PMRF. Because of the heavy costs of the missile Star Wars program, it looks like President Obama will be cutting its budget heavily. I read in the paper recently that PMRF is leasing "launchings" to foreign countries who want to test out the capabilities of their missiles.

The most important lesson I learned was "IN UNITY, THERE IS STRENGTH."

The third civil disobedience action I participated in was eight years ago when the homeless in Hawai'i decided to march from Ala Moana Park to City Hall. About eighty people participated in this peaceful march at 9 p.m. to call attention to the fact that the homeless had no place to go, especially during the forty days and nights of nonstop rain that Oahu was experiencing. Some of the homeless started to pitch their tents in front of the fountain near the entrance to City Hall.

Police arrived at the scene and instructed all of us demonstrators to remove our tents and stay on the sidewalks; otherwise, we would be arrested. When everyone did what the police instructed, all the TV media started to pack up to leave. They were not interested in covering a nonstory. Utu Langi, one of the organizers of the march, saw what was happening and decided to keep the media on scene by disobeying the police. He went in front of the fountain and lay down as though to sleep. After a few minutes, a few of us decided that Utu needed company, so five of us joined Utu.

However, the police took away a Micronesian youth, saying he was too young to be arrested and another Micronesian mother holding a baby was dissuaded from sitting in front of the fountain because of the infant in her arms. In the end, only four of us were sitting or lying in front of the fountain.

Fortunately, I put out an URGENT call to my son to pack his gear and quickly come to video our civil disobedience action. I also instructed him to bring some bail money with him. When he arrived, he immediately began shooting this very peaceful demonstration and showed how the arrests were also very peaceful.

The next morning, the civil disobedience action was on the front page of the main dailies and on all the TV news.

Utu and I were released from our cells after one or two hours; the other two had to stay overnight in their cells because one of them went limp, which represented "resisting arrest," and, therefore, could not be bailed out. The fourth person had a warrant on her because of unpaid fines, so she also could not be bailed out that night.

Arriving at the downtown Honolulu police station, I noticed that my son had already arrived before us. I was much relieved, hoping that he could bail us out immediately. The authorities had another plan—they decided that we needed to experience being in a cell block for at least one or two hours. When the very thick cell door slammed shut, I felt claustrophobic and wondered how long I could last in the cell. Every minute seemed like an eternity to me. But it was worth it.

The next morning, I received a phone call from the pastor of Kawaiaha'o United Church of Christ—a church I had been attending. Rev. Kekuna asked what he could do from his end to support our action. I responded by saying, "Open up the fellowship hall of the church." The congregation responded in great support and most of the homeless who had participated in the march were accommodated—not only with a place to sleep, but with breakfasts, dinners, and even packed lunches. I felt the strong spirit of the congregation as it was "elevated" during this period of great service to the community.

Governor Linda Lingle also rose to the challenge and started emergency shelters within one month of the demonstration.

The opening of shelters was a temporary fix; there are still many homeless in Hawai'i, who are seeking permanent affordable housing. After living in shelters for months and years, where do families go, especially large families with low wage earners? From my perspective, this is the number one dilemma faced in Hawai'i today. Studio apartments now go for an average of around $1,000 month, one bedroom for around $1,500, and so on. Because land is limited in paradise, only the rich seem to be able to move here with their millions. A very sad situation indeed.

Lesson learned: The ACLU is very helpful when one is involved in peaceful action for the rights of people, especially the right to demonstrate and the right to have a roof over your family. Also having a video of the peaceful demonstration was key in ACLU's success in clearing our records. In addition, we were compensated by the City of Honolulu for abridging our rights as taxpayers in Honolulu since the demonstration was not on private property. It was the most money I have earned for one hour in a cell. One can google Honolulu ACLU actions five or six years ago to find the details of the settlement online.

Another important lesson: Try not to do civil disobedience action when there are only four of you participating...the bigger the number of people willing to be arrested, the better it is for the arrestees.

Finally, I want to add some "Breaking News," which validates why it is so important to stand up for what we believe in and especially others' rights. A recent study by Oxfam (reported January 22, 2014) revealed that eighty-five people (that's people, not percent) control as much wealth as the bottom 3.5 billion people in the world. Furthermore, in November 2013, the World Economic Forum ranked the widening income disparities as the second greatest worldwide risk in the next twelve to eighteen months. It is truly unthinkable that eighty-five individuals can control as much wealth as the bottom 3.5 billion people.... We all need to pray and meditate on this matter and seek inspiration for ways to address this unbelievable truth in our midst. This is not the Lord's kingdom on earth that Jesus taught us to pray for.

To find out more about the growing economic disparities in our world, I recommend you see the groundbreaking new film, *Inequality for All*, produced by filmmaker Jacob Kornbluth and featuring Robert Reich, a Berkeley professor, best-selling author, and Clinton cabinet member. Visit www.

InequalityforAll.com for details on where you can see it or purchase a copy.

"Ke Akua
Hallowed be Thy Name
Thy Kingdom Come,
Thy Will be done
on Earth as it is in Heaven."

— Jesus in the Lord's Prayer

People of Okinawa and U.S. Bases

I am asking my readers to sign the following petition to ask that a new military base not be built at Henoko. I have visited Okinawa five times and have had a tour of schools and homes located right next to U.S. military bases. In talking with residents of the area, I learned that the U.S. military bases have had a significant negative impact on civilians living close by. Since 1972, 120 American planes have crashed on Okinawa; at least one crash-landed into an elementary school, killing several children. Errant howitzer shells have caused forest fires, soil erosion, and earth tremors. U.S. military personnel commit about 1,000 crimes a year, including the highly-publicized rape of a twelve-year old girl by three Marines in 1995. American weapons systems, possibly including nuclear weapons, have left toxic pollutants in the earth and waters around Okinawa. Presently, military bases take up 20 percent of the land in Okinawa (in Hawai'i U.S. military bases also take up 20 percent of Hawai'i's land).

As an Okinawan-American, I cannot idly stand by and watch U.S. military presence poison the lives of the people, rape children and women, crash into schools, and take up valuable land that is much needed for affordable housing. Please support the people of Okinawa (and Hawai'i) as they ask for their land back for affordable housing, schools, parks, and community centers. Thank you.

STATEMENT

We oppose construction of a new US military base within Okinawa, and support the people of Okinawa in their struggle for peace, dignity, human rights and protection of the environment.

We the undersigned oppose the deal made at the end of 2013 between Prime Minister Shinzo Abe and Governor of Okinawa Hirokazu Nakaima to deepen and extend the military colonization of Okinawa at the expense of the people and the environment. Using the lure of economic development, Mr. Abe has extracted approval from Governor Nakaima to reclaim the water off Henoko, on the northeastern shore of Okinawa, to build a massive new U.S. Marine air base with a military port.

Plans to build the base at Henoko have been on the drawing board since the 1960s. They were revitalized in 1996, when the sentiments against U.S. military bases peaked following the rape of a twelve-year-old Okinawan child by three U.S. servicemen. In order to pacify such sentiments, the U.S. and Japanese governments planned to close Futenma Marine Air Base in the middle of Ginowan City and move its functions to a new base to be constructed at Henoko, a site of extraordinary bio-diversity and home to the endangered marine mammal dugong.

Governor Nakaima's reclamation approval does not reflect the popular will of the people of Okinawa. Immediately before the gubernatorial election of 2010, Mr. Nakaima, who had previously accepted the new base construction plan, changed his position and called for relocation of the Futenma base outside the prefecture. He won the election by defeating a candidate who had consistently opposed the new base. Polls in recent years have shown that 70 to 90 percent of the people of Okinawa opposed the Henoko base plan. The poll conducted immediately after Nakaima's recent reclamation approval showed that 72.4 percent of the people of Okinawa saw the governor's decision as a "breach of his election pledge." The reclamation approval was a betrayal of the people of Okinawa.

73.8 percent of the U.S. military bases (those for exclusive U.S. use) in Japan are concentrated in Okinawa, which is only .6 percent of the total land mass of Japan. 18.3 percent of the Okinawa Island is occupied by the U.S. military. Futenma Air Base originally was built during the 1945 Battle of Okinawa by U.S. forces in order to prepare for battles on the mainland of Japan. They simply usurped the land from local residents. The base should have been returned to its owners after the war, but the U.S. military has retained it even though now almost seven decades have passed. Therefore, any conditional return of the base is fundamentally unjustifiable.

The new agreement would also perpetuate the long suffering of the people of Okinawa. Invaded in the beginning of the 17th century by Japan and annexed forcefully into the Japanese nation at the end of the 19th century, Okinawa was in 1944 transformed into a fortress to resist advancing U.S. forces and thus to buy time to protect the Emperor System. The Battle of Okinawa killed more than 100,000 local residents, about a quarter of the island's population. After the war, more bases were built under the U.S. military occupation. Okinawa "reverted" to Japan in 1972, but the Okinawans' hope for the removal of the military bases was shattered. Today, people of Okinawa continue to suffer from crimes and accidents, high decibel aircraft noise and environmental pollution caused by the bases. Throughout these decades, they have suffered what the U.S. Declaration of Independence denounces as "abuses and usurpations," including the presence of foreign "standing armies without the consent of our legislatures."

Not unlike the 20th century U.S. Civil Rights struggle, Okinawans have non-violently pressed for the end to their military colonization. They tried to stop live-fire military drills that threatened their lives by entering the exercise zone in protest; they formed human chains around military bases to express their opposition; and about a hundred thousand people, one tenth of the population, have turned out periodically for massive demonstrations. Octogenarians initiated the campaign to prevent the construction of the Henoko base with a sit-in that has been continuing for years. The prefectural assembly passed resolutions to oppose the Henoko base plan. In January 2013, leaders of all the 41 municipalities of Okinawa signed the petition to the government to remove the newly deployed MV-22 Osprey from Futenma base and to give up the plan to build a replacement base in Okinawa.

We support the people of Okinawa in their non-violent struggle for peace, dignity, human rights, and protection of the environment. The Henoko marine base project must be canceled and Futenma returned forthwith to the people of Okinawa.

January 2014

Norman Birnbaum, Professor Emeritus, Georgetown University

Herbert Bix, Emeritus Professor of History and Sociology, State University of New York at Binghamton

Reiner Braun, Co-president International Peace Bureau and Executive Director of International Association of Lawyers Against Nuclear Arms

Noam Chomsky, Professor Emeritus of Linguistics, Massachusetts Institute of Technology

John W. Dower, Professor Emeritus of History, Massachusetts Institute of Technology

Alexis Dudden, Professor of History, University of Connecticut

Daniel Ellsberg, Senior Fellow at the Nuclear Age Peace Foundation, former Defense and State Department official

Richard Falk, Milbank Professor of International Law Emeritus, Princeton University

John Feffer, Co-director of Foreign Policy In Focus (www.fpif.org) at the Institute for Policy Studies

Norma Field, Professor Emerita, East Asian Languages and Civilizations, University of Chicago

Bruce Gagnon, Coordinator of the Global Network Against Weapons & Nuclear Power in Space

Joseph Gerson (Ph.D.), Director, Peace & Economic Security Program, American Friends Service Committee

Kate Hudson (Ph.D.), General Secretary, Campaign for Nuclear Disarmament

Naomi Klein, Author and journalist

Joy Kogawa, Author of *Obasan*

Peter Kuznick, Professor of History, American University

Catherine Lutz, Professor of Anthropology and International Studies, Brown University

Kyo Maclear, Writer and Children's Author

Mairead Maguire, Nobel Peace laureate

Kevin Martin, Executive Director, Peace Action

Gavan McCormack, Professor Emeritus, Australian National University

Michael Moore, Filmmaker

Steve Rabson, Professor Emeritus, Brown University/Veteran, United States Army, Henoko, Okinawa, 1967-68

Mark Selden, a Senior Research Associate in the East Asia Program at Cornell University

Oliver Stone, Filmmaker

David Vine, Associate Professor of Anthropology, American University

The Very Rev. the Hon. Lois Wilson, Former President, World Council of Churches

Lawrence Wittner, Professor Emeritus of History, State University of New York/Albany

Ann Wright, Retired U.S. Army Colonel and former U.S. diplomat

(In the alphabetical order of family names, as of January 7, 2014)

To Sign the Petition, please visit:
closethebase.org/take-action

Micronesia and the Solomon Report

The following information is taken from a pamphlet titled "Micronesia and the Solomon Report" and is reprinted here with permission from Micronesians United.

I think it is important to include this short brochure because probably 99.9 percent of the U.S. population is unaware that such a secret report exists. As mentioned in the brochure, only portions of the Solomon Report and only sanitized portions of it saw the light of day. And most Micronesians themselves have been denied their own history. In the future perhaps, Micronesian students will be able to read the entire Solomon Report as part of their senior year course or university course. It is important for colonized people to be freed of their colonized past by understanding their own history and undoing the internalized racism that is part of being colonized peoples. I, myself, am trying to deal with "internalized racism" accumulated over the years and in different places where I have lived and worked.

The islands of Micronesia have had a long history of colonialism. In 1986 the Federated States of Micronesia (FSM) and the Republic of the Marshall Islands (RMI) gained independence under the Compact of Free Association with the U.S. (COFA)

Although somewhat divided by differences in language and customs, the Micronesian nation states are united by their exposure to U.S. colonialism and its nuclear bomb experimentation before and after World War II, amounting to the same as 1.6 Hiroshima bombs being detonated every day for 12 years (*New York Times*).

Micronesia has been subjected to U.S. control since 1947, when it became a U.S. Trust Territory. But by the 1960s Micronesians were developing their own Congress, and the U.S. was in danger of losing the islands for its strategic military value as a stepping stone to Asia.

So in 1963, the Solomon Report was commissioned by President Kennedy to determine how to make U.S. colonialism in Micronesia appealing to Micronesians at a time when they craved a move towards independence.

Although U.S. officials claim that the Report does not represent policy, it does, in fact, put forth U.S. policy.

The Solomon Report really asked: How can the U.S. control Micronesia cheaply and effectively? The Solomon Report to this day remains mostly "confidential." Only the sanitized version has been released.

This pamphlet was created by Micronesians United with the assistance of Univ. of Hawai'i student, Kara Hisatake. Photo taken from the Micronesian Seminar Photo Archive at www.micsem.org/photos.

The Scariest Story

I have avoided writing this chapter until the last moment because my stomach turns every time I try to tell the story of what happened in Micronesia when the U.S. exploded sixty-seven atomic and nuclear bombs in Bikini and Enewetak, culminating with the largest bomb of all—the BRAVO bomb, detonated in the atmosphere on March 1, 1954. BRAVO was a full-fledged hydrogen bomb that was 1,000 times more powerful than the weapon that had devastated Hiroshima nine years earlier. It created a radioactive cloud that plumed over 7,000 square miles—about the size of New Jersey.

According to a PBS broadcast, the BRAVO bomb went twenty-five miles into the stratosphere. When it exploded in that stratospheric sphere, the radiation fallout did not come straight down. The radiation spread all over the Pacific and covered the Marshall Islands, Pohnpei, Chu'uk, Kosrae, Yap, Palau, parts of the Philippines, and probably radiated hundreds, if not thousands, of islands in the Pacific. Significant radiation was even detected in Canada and other parts of the world. Yet the true story of the impact of BRAVO on the peoples, the land, and the waters of the Pacific has been deliberately kept out of sight and mind from the general population of the United States.

Beverly Keever, a journalism professor at the University of Hawai'i in Manoa, did a masterful job of investigative reporting in her book *News Zero: The New York Times and the Bomb*.

As Keever points out in her book, the adverse effects of radiation and radioactivity on the people's health and environment were virtually ignored or even denied by the U.S. government in public announcements and were given miniscule coverage in the *New York Times*. In fact, the *Times* did more than commit the sin of omission when its reporter William L. Laurence and the photo-editing staff covered up the government's lie about the absence of radiation at the Trinity test site and thus misled readers.

March 1, 2014 is the sixtieth anniversary of BRAVO. Yet no reporters in the U.S. seem to be willing to cover this most significant anniversary. Why is there so much silence about the sixtieth anniversary of one of the most significant events that have impacted, and will continue to impact, the lives of millions of people throughout the world? The radioactivity of plutonium lives on for 500,000 years, thus adding to the present and future peril for our planet.

I attended the fiftieth anniversary of BRAVO in the Marshall Islands on March 1, 2004, along with representatives from a few religious bodies. There were a handful of reporters from Europe and Japan, but no major reporters from the U.S. mainstream press. The survivors of BRAVO, called ERUB (Enewetak, Rongelap, Utrik, and Bikini), tried their best to get the world to pay attention to their plight but to no avail.

I encourage everyone to pick up Beverly Keever's book, *News Zero*. It is the scariest story ever told; I could hardly finish reading the first chapter without shivering. I hope there are some brave souls willing and ready to hear the truth about the sixty-seven bombs detonated in the Pacific, which will continue to affect many (if not most) of our lives in the present and into the future.

I also admire Adam Horowitz for his service to the world in producing an awe-inspiring and terrifying account of the secrecy behind the U.S. nuclear program in Micronesia. The film, *Nuclear Savage*, demonstrates how the United States government used Marshall Islanders as human guinea pigs for more than three decades in order to study the effects of radiation on human beings.

The film raises questions of racism and why the U.S. government continues to cover up the real story behind the explosion of sixty-seven atomic and nuclear bombs in the Marshall Islands and the Pacific Ocean and focuses on the Project 4.1 human experimental project.

Using recently declassified United States government documents and survivor testimonies, *Nuclear Savage* reveals one of the most disturbing chapters in U.S. history on how Marshall Islanders, labeled as "savages" by those in power, were deliberately used as human guinea pigs.

Teachers and professors at all levels of society are encouraged to show this film in educational settings so the truth will come out and justice will prevail in the end.

This increased awareness is desperately needed as revealed by Giff Johnson in a recent article titled, "We're Just Going to Wait for These People to Die" about the Baker atomic test at Bikini in 1946, which was the second test detonated at Bikini following World War II.

Johnson writes that, "Bad faith negotiations by the U.S. government produced a flawed nuclear compensation settlement in the Marshalls." Petitions from the Marshall Islands for compensation for nuclear weapons testing damages have languished for years. Because no formal response has come from the U.S. Congress or Obama Administration, New York Congressman, Gary Ackerman, angrily commented during a 2010 public hearing:

The Marshall Islands "claim" we owe (them) US$2 billion and so what? We're going to just wait for these people to die, right? We've given cancer to them, taken away their property…. They've put a value on it, and it seems to me that if we know that this is about dignity, then there has to be something besides "good luck fellows" with whatever few years you might have left…. You can't unscrew them is the point. But we do compensate people for wrongs that we've committed. I know we're doing some stuff, and I know we spent half a billion bucks pretending to do the right thing, but they deserve to be compensated. What we did was inhuman and unconscionable.

Johnson notes that fifty-five years after the last test was conducted, many documents remain classified, which means the people of the Marshall Islands are left unaware of the full ramifications of the nuclear weapons tests at Bikini and Enewetak.

Johnson concludes by asking:

What does the future hold? Unless the Marshall Islands takes up the challenge to gain U.S. Congress support for expanded compensation and medical programs with an organized and systematic campaign of action, there is little hope that the U.S. Congress will ever on its own resolve the U.S. government's nuclear test legacy that continues to be a black mark on the relationship between the two countries.

I encourage you to google "Nuclear Savage" and rent the film. After seeing the film, please let me know what actions you were able to take (such as showing the film to more and more people and groups. Out of this kind of education, it is hoped that "outraged" or "empathetic" U.S. citizens will put pressure on their elected representatives in Congress to take action on the Changed Circumstances petition from the Marshall Islands government. This petition, asking for more just compensation, for more free health services (now especially for children and grandchildren of survivors who are experiencing second and third generations of leukemia and other illnesses) and a request to fix the Enewetak Dome (which is cracking and emitting radiation) has been languishing in Congress for at least the last thirteen years.

Marshallese survivors plan strategy for 50th anniversary of
BRAVO bomb, March 1, 2004.

Part Four

HEALTH IS EVERYTHING

"Be a treasure to the poor, an admonisher to
the rich, an answerer of the cry of the needy, a
preserver of the sanctity of thy pledge. Be fair
in thy judgment, and guarded in thy speech."

"Be as a lamp unto them that walk in darkness,
a joy to the sorrowful, a sea for the thirsty, a
haven for the distressed, an upholder and de-
fender of the victim of oppression."

"Say: no man can attain his true station except
through his justice. No power can exist except
through unity. No welfare and no well-being
can be attained except through consultation."

— Baha'u'llah

Living to Be 128 Years Old!

It is amazing how most of us have been programmed to think that we should not live beyond 100 years. The comments I receive when I indicate that my goal is to live to be 128 years old with mind and body intact indicate a "closed" mind to living a fruitful life beyond 100. Some friends think it is "obscene" even to want to live beyond 100; others feel there is no such thing as being productive in the years beyond 100. I think differently because of role models from around the world who lead productive lives by serving the community and sharing their wisdom that comes with age.

In Judaism, the phrase "May you live to be 120 years old" is a common blessing. And many rabbis have been productive beyond 100. Jeanne Clement of France lived to be 122 years old and is the oldest documented person in the *Guinness World Records*. The next two are women from the United States, who lived to be 119 and 117. The United States has the greatest number of known centenarians with 53,364, according to 2010 records. Japan is expected to have 272,000 centenarians by 2050, or one per 3,522 people, according to Wikipedia. Just recently, Japan's Jiroemon Kimura died at the age of 116. He was born on April 19, 1897, when Queen Victoria still reigned over the British Empire.

Instead of thinking of centenarians as a burden to society and a burden to the Social Security system, many of us in the Mokichi Okada Association (MOA), which I'll talk more about shortly, believe that it is desirable to live long productive lives, through comprehensive and holistic practices of appreciating art, doing flower arrangements, yoga, healing energy work (OPT), nature farming, tea ceremony, cooking nutritious meals, and the list goes on. Central to all of this is the importance of "service." Just imagine a society where centenarians and beyond were actively involved in justice and peace work, utilizing their wisdom. Perhaps there will come a day when there are no wars because of the shared wisdom of centenarians in our midst.

The May 2013 *National Geographic* cover depicted the face of a baby with the following statement, "This baby will live to be 120." Gradually, people's thinking is changing to include the possibility of a long and fruitful life with wise persons helping to build a better world for all.

This morning (January 28, 2014) I received the following email from Evolving Wisdom. Since so many of my older friends are struggling with how to keep their brains fresh and working, I want to share one excerpt from it with you about the free online seminars Evolving Wisdom offers:

Our friends at the National Institute for the Clinical Application of Behavioral Medicine (NICABM) have once again brought together **leading experts** in the field of brain science to show you all the ways you can use those latest discoveries to enhance your own brain power.

Here are just a few of the **free** seminars they'll be offering every Wednesday during their 5th Annual Online Series:

"Epigenetics: What Really Controls Our Genes and Why We Don't Have to Be Victims of Our DNA," with Bruce Lipton, Ph.D.

"Happiness and Neuroplasticity: Simple Strategies for Rewiring Your Brain," with Rick Hanson, Ph.D.

"Focus: Why Concentration Can Make Your Brain More Powerful," with Daniel Goleman, Ph.D.

Google "Evolving Wisdom" and you will have access to many of their ongoing free seminars throughout the year.

Recently, I met my friend Nia Aitaoto for breakfast at Down to Earth. Nia is my "networker," who is lining up speaking engagements for me from now until ten years into the future, using my book as my platform.

We talked about how we would live to be 128 years old; Nia is about twenty years younger than I. We talked about how we wanted to enter the next world at age 128. When I told her the real story of how my friend, Maryanne Takagi of Oakland, California, was healthy one day and the next day was dead from natural causes, Nia insisted that I share this true story with all my readers. Many of you who knew Maryanne Takagi will verify the truth of this story.

Maryanne was a Nisei activist who had many friends. One night she was "talking story" on the telephone with one of her best friends. Her husband, Paul Takagi—a well-known criminologist who taught at U.C.-Berkeley—was reading downstairs in his study and heard the laughter upstairs. Suddenly, there was a big "thump" from upstairs. When he went to find out the cause of this loud noise, he found Maryanne was lying on the floor, with the phone hanging loosely from its stand; Maryanne was already dead from a massive heart attack or aneurysm. Maryanne left this world laughing so hard with her girlfriend, who was also laughing hard on the other end. Her friend survived to tell the story. If one had a choice, wouldn't we all want to be so pleasantly surprised?

Ola

Why is this section of my book titled "Health is Everything"? My mother, who was active until she died at age ninety-six, would often tell me in Japanese that "Health is everything." She emphasized that when one is ill, the whole world looks dark. Therefore, when I saw an announcement for a film titled *Ola: Health is Everything* being shown at the Monday night film café, I immediately thought of my mother's comment.

When my friend Diane Lee Pilla and I saw *Ola*, however, I realized it had a deeper meaning beyond "Health is the most important thing in life," as stated by my mother. Matthew Nagato, the writer and producer of the film, with assistance from the Hawai'i Primary Care Association, discussed how many social determinants factor into being healthy as an individual and as a community. When one talks about healthy communities and healthy individuals, one is talking about quality education from preschool through high school and beyond, adequate housing, a living wage, spirituality, nature farming, less stress, nutrition, a healthy lifestyle, complementary medicine, beauty, art, music, exercise, service, a positive self-identity, having meaning in life, interdependence, forgiveness, sharing, and the list goes on and on. In this sense, health is everything; it is not only the Western medical system that should define what matters in discussing health issues.

As Norman Oshiro often describes in his lectures at the Mokichi Okada Association, "We wake up in the morning and brush our teeth with toothpaste that has chemicals in it; we wash our hair and scalp with shampoo and conditioners that have toxic chemicals in them; we drive to work in traffic that causes much stress; we work at jobs that are often not fulfilling and the environment at work may be stressful; one's pay does not provide enough income to pay for adequate housing, dental care, vision care; our children attend schools where music, art, and P.E. are being cut from the classroom; food in the cafeteria is not healthy, everyone comes home tired and stressed, and the doctors prescribe anti-depressants for our children, our youth, our parents, and ourselves." Of course, there are so many other environmental and social issues that we can add to this list. In the real world, especially at the grassroots level, health is everything. The higher the income, the more choices we have for leading a healthier lifestyle.

In Hawai'i alone, $9 billion is spent on the health care system. Are people in Hawai'i healthier because of such a large expenditure of state and federal funds? The consensus response for the most part is "No." In fact, the state of our health is worsening, both in Hawai'i and nationally.

I was fortunate to have grown up in Hawai'i in the 1940s and 1950s when health care was not such a profit-driven system. I don't recall ever being prescribed any antibiotics or medicines during the entire twenty-one years I lived in Wahiawa before I left for Claremont, California to do graduate studies. Having been "drug-free" during my formative years, I am shocked at how much the pharmaceutical companies push drugs in television ads, magazine ads, billboards, and almost everywhere I look. It seems that prescription drugs became a part of one's growing up environment from the 1960s on, and especially once Kaiser introduced a new kind of insurance system—the health maintenance organization

(HMO), emanating from its hospital in Oakland, California. The concept sounded good for containing costs, but the reality led to a more and more profit-driven medical system.

Since I was living in Oakland, California, in the 1960s, I felt the changes in health care gradually move from preventive care and primary care to maintenance of chronic illnesses through specialized diagnoses and services. The root causes of illnesses were not being addressed, and a patient was not being seen as a "whole" person who lived in a certain kind of environment at home, school, and work. Since my mother or father did not go to doctors for regular checkups, I grew up thinking this was normal. Even today at seventy-three years old, I have not visited any doctors, except for prenatal care and when giving birth at Alta Bates Hospital to my son Bob. Instead, I go to the firehouse in my neighborhood once a year to say, "Hi" and have my blood pressure taken. Two years ago, I had a skin problem so I visited MOA, a health and wellness clinic in Honolulu, and visited with Leon Garcia, a Western-trained doctor who volunteers at the clinic. He believes in complementary medicine, so he listened to my wish for only natural solutions and encouraged me to continue what I was already doing—Okada Purifying Therapy (OPT). Between taking doTerra medicinal oils and OPT, I was able to heal myself.

On the ride home from seeing *Ola: Health is Everything*, Diane and I reflected on the film and agreed that *Ola* was a great gift from the hearts of the film's writer and producers to the people of Hawai'i and the rest of the world. In order for our state to move toward "prevention" and "healthy communities," the real world issues of poverty, equal access to quality education from pre-school through college, racism, military toxins, lifestyles, access to organic fruits, vegetables and meats at affordable prices, new immigrants who don't speak English, urban pollution, and other related issues all need to be addressed. And the film, *Ola*, also stressed the importance of service to the community—of giving back to those in need. Children and youth who were interviewed for *Ola*, stressed the importance of "service" as a key factor in their happiness, sense of self-worth, and becoming better students.

Ola (a Hawaiian word which means life, well being) honors the heritage received from our host culture—Kanaka Maoli (Native Hawaiian) culture—and demonstrates that the path to a healthy, sustainable future for Hawai'i is found in the host culture's oldest, most cherished values.

For more information about *Ola: Health Is Everything*, visit:
www.olamovie.com

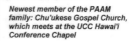

Newest member of the PAAM family: Chu'ukese Gospel Church, which meets at the UCC Hawai'i Conference Chapel

Leadership Team: Sinbad Michael, Roy Hamrick, Senior Pastor Matai Silo, Graceful Enlet, Ermes Siales, Jano Ruben

Liwina Phillip, Eruko Phillip, Ketsen Hanrick, Enita Ilon

www.olamovie.com

ola

health is everything

the journey

These heroes show us,
by example, the power
of communities to
heal themselves.

WE ALMOST MISSED OUR FLIGHT. It was early, maybe 3:00 a.m., just another day of
filming on another neighbor island; the kind of exhausted day when you find yourself on auto pilot.
Until the moment you step behind the camera, it's hard to understand how involved making a movie
is. How a thousand little details mean everything. And so it was that morning, when I saw through
bleary eyes that we were about to fly to the wrong town, with no time to make the correct flight. It was
in that moment that I realized filmmaking is not only a surreal experience, it's one you have to love
deeply in order to make it through mornings like that.

You also have to love the subject of your movie,
to care about the message you're conveying
through words and images and sound. That kind
of emotional investment doesn't come easily, and
I know that as much as I enjoyed this experience,
it's not every day that a subject comes along and
captivates you enough to go through the grueling
process of turning an idea into a movie.

When this film was first proposed, I wasn't very
interested in doing it. Health care documentaries
can be dark and scary things. The sky, after all, is
falling. The health care system is collapsing and
everyone is trying to fix something that seems on
the surface to be beyond repair.

So, to make a film about social 'determinants'
- one of those words that sounds vague but
also ominous - and tell people that in order
to be healthy we had to address...Poverty?
Homelessness? Equity? Education? Now that was
a scary idea.

Ultimately, it was the people who appear in our
film that changed my perspective. I came to
realize very quickly that what these heroes are
doing in their towns is more than just affecting
social issues or the health of people who live

there. They are showing us, by example, the
simple power of communities to heal themselves.

I admire and have deep affection for everyone
who welcomed us into their communities and
into their lives. I hope we've done justice to their
work while telling a compelling story about
how interdependent we are. I am also eternally
grateful to my dedicated crew, without whom this
simply would not have been possible.

It is a privilege to live among the gifts that make
Hawai'i such a unique, special place, and I
wanted to ensure that this film was a love letter to
our islands; culturally, visually, and emotionally.
Because of those gifts, in the midst of scarcity
we found abundance, in the midst of anguish we
found joy, and in the midst of hardship we found
hope. We found that health is everything.

In the end, we were able to get on the correct
flight that morning. Which means that somehow,
the Universe wanted to get this film made. It's
hard to catch lightning in a bottle, or to have
lightning strike twice but, with your help,
perhaps we can do this again.

matthew nagato
PRODUCER

Health and Solidarity

Matthew Nagato, the writer of Ola, recently gave a TED talk health in terms of cultivating community. As I mentioned earlier, I'm a believer in solidarity, and solidarity is especially important in terms of our health care. If we wish to improve health care for all of us, we must work together to do so. You can listen to Matthew's talk at:

https://www.youtube.com/watch?v=vaaZSRegffs

When I recently spoke to Matthew about solidarity, he shared with me the following:

> I think part of the reason many people struggle with solidarity is a widespread lack of empathy. As we all grapple with the incredible challenges around us—whether it's making a living, being healthy, finding happiness, or simply experiencing peace—it's easier to revert to our baser instincts (survivalism, individualism) than it is to make the sacrifices needed to manifest true solidarity with others. Part of this, in my view, is the result of our culture, which doesn't celebrate collectivism but, rather, the triumph of individual achievements over the benefit of others.
>
> I don't know how we manifest greater solidarity with others on a larger, societal scale, because the consciousness of society is so fragmented and sensitive now. I am a true

believer, however, in doing what you can for the situation directly in front of you. To cultivate solidarity on the micro level—be it within a family first, then a neighborhood—and hopefully others will do the same.

As Matthew suggests, I invite you to start small, where you are and within your family, and then expand, or maybe you even want to take a big leap of faith right away to make dynamic changes in this world. Either way, I encourage you to find ways people can come together to make our health, our society, our world a better place.

Dr. Kekuni Blaisdell

Lynette Cruz, Julia Estrella, and Ron Fujiyoshi.
(Kekuni in chair)

Richard Kekuni Akana Blaisdell was a professor of medicine at the University of Hawai'i, in Honolulu and was a co-founder of E Ola Mau, an organization of Hawaiian health profession-als. He was also the convener of the Pro-Hawaiian Sovereignty Working Group and coordinator of Ka Pakaukau, a group of twelve organizations seeking independence for Hawai'i. This book is dedicated to Dr. Kekuni Blaisdell. He also worked to organize the Peoples' International Tribunal, Hawai'i 1993. This Tribunal, named Ka Ho'okolokolonui Kanaka Maoli, was an event where the United States and the state of Hawai'i were put on trial for crimes against the Hawaiian people, the Kanaka Maoli. (I speak about it further in my chapter in this book about Oscar Lopez Rivera.)

Dr. Blaisdell was part of a panel on "Pu'uhonua in Hawaiian Culture" sponsored by Kahua Na'auao on August 24, 1991. Below are excerpts from Dr. Blaisdell's presentation on traditional Kanaka Maoli healing practices. It was published in whole as an article in *In Motion Magazine* on April 28, 1996 and is excerpted with permission.

Dr. Kekuni Blaisdell is known more for his organizing work around 'Kanaka Maoli self-determination and not as well known for his work in the area of indigenous healing practices and indigenous healing plants. Thus this article is informative of Dr. Blaisdell's passion for restoring the health of his people using the wisdom of his ancestors and using gifts from Mother Nature.

Traditional lapa'au (Kanaka Maoli healing practices)

In all of Polynesia, only in Hawai'i were there such heiau ho'ola for: (1) training of haumana (students) with a rigorous 20-year or so curriculum; (2) research, with development of simple surgery, fracture-setting, clyster enema, thermo-heliotherapy, and la'au (medicinal plants); (3) special practices, such as cultivation, gathering and preparation of la'au (medicines), ho'ohapai and ho'ohanau keiki (induction of pregnancy and baby-delivery), pa'ao'ao (child care), 'o'o (simple surgery), h-ah-a (palpation), lomilomi (massage), ha'iha'i iwi

(bone-setting), ka'alawa maka and 'ike lihilihi (close observation), k-ahea and makani (calling and engaging spiritual
forces); 'ana'ana, kuni and ho'opi'opi'o (engaging adverse and
counter-adverse forces).

Pu'uhonua (sanctuaries) contained healing power and were
of several varieties: (1) sacred sites, such as Pu'uhonua o
Honaunau, which included the home of the ruling ali'i
(chief) and adjacent heiau which housed the iwi (bones) of
previous ruling chiefs, and Kukaniloko, ali'i birthing place
in Wahiawa, O'ahu;' (2) the ruling ali'i himself, such as
Kamehameha, and specified members of his court, such as
Ka'ahumanu; (3) ho'ola kanawai (sacred healing laws), such as
kanawai mamalahoe; and (4) Pohaku o K-ane (stone of Kane)
for each 'ohana (family).

The above-described highly-organized, yet locally-based
system was threatened in 1778 by the fatal impact of epidem-
ics of foreign contagious infections, beginning with gonorrhea,
syphilis, tuberculosis, then pneumonia, influenza, measles,
mumps, typhoid and other infectious diarrheas, smallpox,
and later leprosy, plague, diphtheria, and streptococcus.

Traditional lapa'au could not stem the devastation. Nor was
Western or Asian medicine effective. Other factors contributing to the over 95% decline in the native population, from an
estimated 800,000 in 1778 to 40,000 in 1893, were: colonial
economic and political exploitation, a market and money economy, private ownership and thus loss of lands, and economic
dependence; repression of kanaka maoli culture, education,
language, and spirituality; cultural conflict, stress and despair;
adoption of harmful foreign ways, such as the use of alcohol

and tobacco, less physical activity, and the Western high-satu-rated fat, high-cholesterol, high-salt and low-fiber diet.

With the U.S. armed invasion of 1893, and the 1898 illegal U.S. annexation and occupation, an official policy of coercive assimilation and de-Hawaiianization ensued with further sup-pression of lapa'au. Although the 1919 Territorial Legislature authorized a Hawaiian Medicine Board to issue licenses to herbalists, two of the three board members were haole who required the kanaka practitioner applicants to use Western scientific names for native medicinal plants in the certifying examination.

In 1965 the examining board was abolished because the stat-ute authorizing it and licensure of traditional practitioners were considered "obsolete." Kanaka Maoli herbalists were no longer recognized, while lomilomi practitioners had to be certified by a separate, albeit still legal, Board of Massage. Thus, kanaka lapa'au practitioners were again compelled to go underground.

Encouraged by E Ola Mau in 1986 and by the 1988 Native Hawaiian Health Care Act, traditional lapa'au healers have re-emerged from "the bush." They have conducted dozens of educational workshops, and are still attempting to organize themselves independently to become officially recognized, develop standards of competence and to pass on their knowl-edge and skills to future generations. These practitioners contend that "akua heals, not the practitioner," that a holistic approach to the entire 'ohana of the patient is necessary, and that spiritual communication is basic. Some practitioners still refuse to accept monetary payment for their services, insisting that theirs is a gift to be shared. Some see "no need" for certification, licensure and liability insurance. They fear control by an imposed foreign government. For the state has arrested la'au-gathering practitioners for "trespassing," and is promoting commercial development, and thus destruction, of our land and ocean resources.

Three options are now apparent: (1) remain underground at the risk of becoming another lost treasure of the old heritage; (2) submit to control by the commerce-oriented, dominant Western society; (3) assert kanaka maoli control of our land and ocean resources. These resources are essential for our livelihood and survival as the first people in our homeland with a distinctive culture in which spiritual affiliation and sharing are paramount rather than individualism, exploitation, materialism, waste and destruction of our natural environment.

Body Wisdom

My mother told me that I screamed my head off and bit her shoulder until it hurt on my first visit to get vaccinated in the Wahiawa office of Dr. Wee. That pretty much describes my relationship with the medical system from that day in 1941 (at age one) to the present day.

Although it was recommended that a student get re-vaccinated at age twelve or thirteen, I refused to visit Dr. Wee. When I attended the Fifth Assembly of the World Council of Churches meeting in Tanzania in 1974 and Kenya in 1975, it was recommended that we be vaccinated against certain diseases. I said, "No."

I have visited twenty-five countries in the past seventy-three years and never received any shots prior to or during any of the trips.

I visited the mile-long slums of Nairobi and had tea served by the residents of that area and visited the villages of Cuba for two or more weeks with no ill effects. The most interesting visit was to the island of Biak in Irian Jaya where our Indonesian Airlines plane was stranded because of a big hole that appeared in the tail of the plane and required an immediate landing. School children lined the roads of each village as we drove by, as though they had not seen such strange animals before. We were given a free all-day tour of the entire island thanks to the wonderful service of Indonesian Air. Since there was nothing available on the island of Biak to repair the plane, the pilot announced at the end of the day that we would proceed to Jakarta on a damaged wing and prayers. Passengers all became fervent believers and cheered loudly when we finally landed safely in Jakarta with emergency vehicles surrounding the landing area.

I credit my stubbornness about Western health care not to stupidity, as my friends insist, or to a careless disregard for a long, healthy life (and I do appreciate the initial childhood vaccinations for serving me well), but to some innate wisdom that I experienced as a four year old. I remember that day very well.

It was an extremely hot and humid morning, and I was standing next to the ironing board while my mother was ironing my best dress for a photo studio visit. I know my mother could not afford a professional studio picture so I am sure our midwife, Mrs. Tanji, had arranged for the free services of her son, who owned the Tanji Photo Studio. My sister was about to enter first grade and I was about to enter kindergarten, so the studio shot was seen as a necessary "kinen" (remembrance).

For someone who had never experienced being ill even for one day, the kinen day was the first time my nose was running profusely and I was feeling miserable. And the humidity in the air and the hot ironing board did not help. Something came upon me at that moment of experiencing misery—I like to call it an epiphany—where my body vowed never to get that sick again. I don't remember most of the days of my life as a toddler or young child, but that kinen day remains a mysterious beacon of truth—something that I refer to as "body wisdom." A wisdom my body has retained to the present day.

Mokichi Okada Association (MOA)

In the same way that some children are born with unexplainable piano abilities, vocal talents, or scientific knowledge, I like to think that I inherited genes for "body wisdom."

Drawn to natural health and wellness programs, I am now a volunteer at a nonprofit wellness organization called the Mokichi Okada Association (MOA), which is located at the corner of South and Queen Streets in Honolulu. The organization was founded by Mokichi Okada (1882-1955), who conducted research on a health program for approximately 30,000 people and established "Purifying Therapy" in 1934 in Tokyo. The MOA Wellness Center is a health care facility based on this model and was first established in 2001 in Tokyo.

In Hawaii, the Church of World Messianity and its Purifying Therapy began in 1953. Today, the church is called Light from the East. The church is a combination of Buddhist and Shinto practices. The nonprofit side of the church was started in 1976 as the Kyusei Kokusai Yuko Shinzenkyokai, later evolving to become the Mokichi Okada Association (MOA) in 1980.

Mokichi Okada healed 20,000 individuals from 1924-1934 with his Okada Purifying Therapy (OPT). In 1935, the Kannon Church was started in Japan, followed by the Health Association also in Japan in 1936.

One interesting story that Mr. Ichikawa, one of MOA's founders, related to me was the story of how Mokichi Okada foresaw the day when one of his disciples would meet President Eisenhower. This disciple, Tomoshige Arashi, was a well-known artist who was invited to do an eleven-city tour of the United States with his artwork. Mokichi Okada had cured Mr. Arashi of an ailment, and thus, the artist became one of Okada's active disciples. Before leaving Japan to begin his eleven-city tour, Mr. Okada told Mr. Arashi that he would meet President Eisenhower during his tour. Mr. Arashi thought it was an impossible thing to have happen on his trip.

That amazing prediction came true when the director of the Rockefeller Foundation attended Mr. Arashi's art show. The director asked whether Mr. Arashi could do a simple portrait of Eisenhower from a picture; when Mr. Arashi produced such a portrait, the director of the foundation showed it to President Eisenhower, who liked the portrait very much. Hence, President Eisenhower asked Mr. Arashi to visit him at his summer White House in Colorado. The visit was supposed to last for five minutes; instead, the exchange was so engaging that the visit turned out to be a twenty-minute conversation. Mokichi Okada was one of the manifestations of God, who could see into the future. His prediction for Mr. Arashi came true in a very amazing way.

Mokichi Okada died in 1955. He is one of God's manifestations who was active in my lifetime since I was fifteen years old in 1955.

One of the highlights of my involvement with MOA happened two years ago when Norman Oshiro, executive director of MOA, led a group to Japan to visit MOA health and wellness centers in various parts of that country. I was fortunate to join the two-week exposure trip, which included stops at natural hot springs in Atami and Hakone, nature farming projects, and two art museums built by Mokichi Okada because art is "medicine." It was heartening indeed to discover that there is a worldwide movement to build centers where people can go to get well "naturally" rather than to Western-style hospitals.

The following is an introduction to the philosophy, history, and practice of the MOA movement:

Today, there are sixteen MOA Wellness Centers worldwide, including Hawai'i and Los Angeles. The centers focus on the following four concepts:

1. a health care that integrates Western Medicine and Complementary and Alternative Medicine
2. a health care that looks at each individual from various points of view
3. a health care that focuses on preventing illness
4. a health care that focuses on human lives in accordance with Nature

The overarching focus is on enhancing spirituality and natural healing ability, i.e. Enhancing Spirit, Mind, and Body.

Lifestyle-related illnesses like cancer, heart disease, and cerebrovascular disease account for 70 percent of the causes of death among all diseases and over 30 percent of the fees for medical treatments. In addition to the people who are seriously threatened by these lifestyle-related illnesses, there is also a surge in the number of people experiencing their preliminary stages. In recent years, problems like Attention Deficit Hyperactive Disorder and Autism have been increasing rapidly among children. Further, mental disorders seem to be increasing in severity.

Limits of Modern Medicine

Many people tend to depend on medical drugs as opposed to changing their lifestyles. However, modern medical care is limited in its focus only on the physical body. If a person's lifestyle improves and the use of medical drugs is minimized, that person will be able to decrease his or her medical expenses.

However, it is not easy to change people's lifestyle in our current social environment where people have been pursing materialistic enrichment and convenience all or most of their lives.

The MOA Wellness Center works with this difficult process of changing people's lifestyles; it studies the physical body, spiritual body, and spirituality, and supports the health of both the body and mind of each individual.

In other words, MOA's goal is for people to obtain a healthy lifestyle that considers not only the way of living but the way of thinking: "Gaining a healthy lifestyle that adjusts to Nature, by realizing and embracing mankind's innate healing ability."

A Solution for Comprehensive Health Care

MOA considers people's lifestyles—including diet, lack of exercise, lack of spiritual connection—and self-centered focus on material abundance, comfort, and convenience as factors contributing to poor health outcomes. Related to this, modern medical care has traditionally focused on alleviating the symptoms of illness rather than the causes, which does not seem to get to the true heart of what is ailing our communities and families.

The MOA Wellness Center offers complementary and alternative medicine to the community that treats not only symptoms, but goes deeper to address health holistically. It is staffed by the "MOA Healthy Life Networks" (the MOA volunteers), in addition to allopathic and alternative medical professionals such as licensed medical doctors, registered nurses, massage therapists, acupuncturists, and naturopathic doctors. By addressing the connection between body, mind, and spirit, MOA's mission is to be a place for holistic spiritual, mental, and physical health. MOA is the only organization in Hawaii that practices integration of all of the healing modalities of energy, manual, alternative, and complementary medicine, exercise, natural foods, and Western Medicine in one program.

MOA Health and Wellness Program

The MOA Wellness Center offers comprehensive care concentrated on teaching people how to become aware of, improve, and make the best use of the natural healing ability inherent in all human beings.

My Personal Testimony about MOA's Effectiveness

In MOA's August 2011 newsletter, I shared the following personal story about how MOA helped me with a health issue:

> I was having my usual lunch at Down to Earth in Moili'ili when a MOA member, Masaki, who was eighty-eight years old, introduced herself and joined my table. We started to

talk about health and wellness, and I shared my goal to live until 128 years since my pastor had a dream where I was still strong in mind and body at that age. Masaki was surprised since Mokichi Okada, the visionary and leader of the MOA health and wellness movement, also wrote that humans in the future would live to a ripe age of 120 plus with mind and body active once health and wellness principles were followed.

Three months later, I ran into Masaki again….she said she had been praying for my health every day since the day she met me. I was so impressed that someone whom I had just met briefly would pray daily for a stranger that I decided to visit the MOA Clinic, where Masaki often visits to do tea ceremony and flower arranging.

I was introduced to the holistic approach of MOA and subsequently went through the purifying therapy training, flower arranging, and tea ceremony. Now, I grow chemical-free vegetables in the small space next to my 350 sq. foot apartment and I hope to support the building of a ryōin (an alternative to a hospital) in Hawaii in the near future.

In March 2011 I came down with "insect-driven" psoriasis. As I write this article in the latter part of July, I am thankful for the five-month experience with pain and suffering via the psoriasis attack. I used the OPT (Okada Purifying Therapy) on myself every night for hours and found the pain and the itch go away gradually. I learned many helpful lessons through this episode, especially the efficacy of OPT to help the body heal more quickly. Since I had a personal experience of using Okada's healing principles, I am more able to introduce the benefits enthusiastically.

MOA Health and Wellness Clinic,
Located on the corner of South and Queen Streets.

MOA Hawai'i staff.

Iatrogenesis

Just a few weeks ago, I learned a new word at MOA—iatrogenesis (originating from a physician). Iatrogenesis or iatrogenic effect refers to preventable harm resulting from medical treatment or advice to patients. In an article and then a book, *Death by Medicine*, Gary Null, Carolyn Dean, Martin Feldman, Debora Rasio, and Dorothy Smith (all either Ph.D. scientists or medical doctors), shared their findings after a review of peer-reviewed journals and government health statistics. They found that the number of unnecessary medical and surgical procedures performed annually is around 7.5 million. And the total number of iatrogenic deaths is around 784,000. Since the 2001 heart disease annual death rate is 699,697 and the cancer death rate is 553,251, these doctors and scientists concluded that the American medical system is the leading cause of death and injury in the United States. This is a bold statement but very believable if one talks to one's friends and relatives. All one needs to do is pick up a daily newspaper and read the story of a supposedly simple procedure that went wrong or hear a story about a patient dying from a stroke after a so-called "successful" operation.

I personally believe the truth of the review because of my own eyewitness account of what happened when my husband had a stroke in 1990 and also by listening to the increasing number of similar stories that seem to be reaching epidemic levels.

When my husband complained of dizziness and nausea, I immediately sensed that it was a stroke because of a warning stroke he'd experienced five years earlier. The doctor who saw Roger in the emergency room was a neurologist. He concluded that the problem was stomach flu; I was told to go home for a couple of hours while liquid was pumped into Roger's body because of possible dehydration. After two hours of waiting, I returned to the emergency room and was told to take Roger home.

As I was dressing him, however, I noticed that he could not sit up, so I asked him how many children he had and he responded "five." Since we only have one child, I knew immediately that this was a stroke and asked for the doctor to return.

The neurologist was upset that I was asking for a cat scan of Roger's brain and peevishly said, "I will call for a cat scan only because you insist." I was told to go home again and return when the results of the cat scan were known—about three hours. When I returned upon receiving a call, I noticed that the nurses looked frantic. The cat scan showed that Roger had undergone a massive brain hemorrhage and had to be sent by ambulance to Redwood City, the only Kaiser facility that could perform the needed surgery, to try to scrape the released blood from the brain. His survival chances, according to the surgeon, were 50-50. After five hours of scraping, Roger went into the intensive care unit. My pastor, Rev. Ben Wu of Sycamore Congregational Church, waited those five agonizing hours with me.

I am always surprised by how fast hospitals try to release patients after major surgery rather than not allow patients to recover sufficiently. Roger was sent home with instructions for steroids to be taken regularly. The steroids took over his nervous system so that Roger could not sit still for even one moment. So my son Bob and I took turns walking Roger around in circles through three rooms. The physician had warned us not to take Roger off the steroids unless we did so very gradually. Sensing that the steroids were the problem and not the cure, and with all three of us not able to sleep at all, I took the drastic measure and immediately stopped the steroid treatment after two days. And much to our surprise, Roger finally was able to fall asleep, and also Bob and me. Then Roger was admitted to the Kaiser Rehabilitation Center in Vallejo, where the staff was experimenting with the Scandinavian method of recovery based on the theory that the more one did physical exercise, the faster the brain recovered. Bob and I stayed at the hospital for twenty-four hours a day for a month and saw the remarkable recovery of many stroke victims; the Scandinavian system was very effective.

After thirty days, however, I was told that Roger was not progressing fast enough so Kaiser could no longer continue rehab services at the site. I was told by Dr. Z that Roger would be permanently disabled for life and he would not be able to return to his work. I was shocked that Dr. Z would give us such a sad prognosis in front of the patient. Why would any doctor want to take away any "hope" from the patient? That still remains a mystery to me.

Fortunately, we did not have long-term medical insurance; otherwise, we might have just accepted the doctor's prognosis. Dr. Z sent us home with the warning that we must at all times hold on to Roger as he moved about.

But as soon as we returned home, we allowed Roger to walk from room to room without help and watched closely as he "banged around" from wall to wall. Finally, he was able to find a new center of equilibrium in his brain through constant practice.

My mother's innate understanding of healing helped me figure out through reflection that the next important step was to get Roger back to work somehow. Knowing that Roger's boss at EG&G was a kind person, we agreed that Roger would sit at his work computer and stay the whole day and let him "feel" his environment as a familiar place. After about two weeks, Roger began to pick at the computer keys and his brain seemed to find new paths to take in recollecting the complex mathematical equations necessary to continue his work. It was truly a miracle. Instead of being permanently disabled, Roger was back to work after two months of leaving Kaiser Rehabilitation.

Marge Bello, a friend, advised us to consider a lawsuit (actually mediation) against Kaiser in Oakland on behalf of Asian Americans who waited long hours at Kaiser emergency because of the stereotype of Asians as always patient and never complaining (and never filing lawsuits). Our communities sometimes have the "shikataganai" (it can't be helped) attitude, so we just accept what comes our way. The neurologist who had made the wrong diagnosis had actually called the day after the incident to apologize. But because we were not thinking of a lawsuit, I had erased that apology. Marge, nonetheless, prodded me to call her lawyer friend to see whether he would be willing to take our case on a contingency basis.

As it turned out, the lawyer was famous in California for donating his time to help in an initiative calling for a statewide single payer health system. Roger and I told Mr. Shear that he could take 40 percent of whatever we won (the maximum allowed in the state) because we believed in the single payer movement, and if we won, we would be helping the movement. Attorney Shear told us the reality that if it were not for Roger having a Ph.D., it would be a hard case to win, but because of the elitist society in which we live, he had a good chance to win. At the same time, because Roger was able to go back to work full-time, the settlement would not be large. After five years of going back and forth with Kaiser, the court date was set. A retired judge was hired to listen to both sides in this mediation system and all the "experts" flew in from San Diego and New York as part of our team.

Attorney Shear knew what it took to win. And he knew that a few hours before midnight prior to the court hearing, negotiators from Kaiser would begin offering settlement deals. And true to form, after much back and forth via phone, we finally agreed to a settlement amount. Both sides really did not want to spend a week in mediation court procedures. The agreement included a proviso that we could not reveal the settlement amount to anyone. But it was enough for us to buy a home in Honokai Hale, Hawai'i, and Roger happily retired from EG&G in 1994.

Kaiser made another mistake in 2001 when Roger went in to check out his broken finger from a fall. Because the computer showed that he had a stroke in 1990, the doctors wanted to make sure that he had not experienced a heart attack. Therefore, the intake physician called for a night of "observation" at the hospital. Knowing how Roger was allergic to most medications, especially aspirin, I asked the doctor to make sure that he did not ingest a blood thinner of any kind. Unfortunately, the intake doctor did not put this key information on the intake form. Sure enough, Roger was given a blood thinner by the attending physician, and that night, he suffered a stroke. It is difficult to recover from a second stroke when one side is already weakened.

Is there a light at the end of the tunnel? Yes, there is a growing movement in Japan and worldwide for an alternative to Western medicine and to hospitals. I was able to visit health and wellness centers in Japan with MOA about three years ago where treatment included music and art therapy, yoga, tea ceremony, flower therapy, and healing energy. Hopefully, Hawai'i MOA will succeed in building a "ryoin," (a holistic healing place) where one can check oneself in for overnight stays in place of a "byoin" (a traditional hospital). This is already happening in Japan and the future looks promising for Hawai'i.

CDC study finds drastic overuse of antibiotics

By Mike Stobbe
Associated Press

NEW YORK >> U.S. doctors are prescribing enough antibiotics to give them to 4 out of 5 Americans every year, an alarming pace that suggests they are being overused, a new government study finds.

Overuse is one reason antibiotics are losing their punch, making infections harder to treat. The report released last week gives the first detailed look at use of these medicines in every state and finds it highest in the South and Appalachia.

"It sounds high," said Keith Rodvold, a professor of pharmacy practice at the University of Illinois at Chicago.

There is no scientific consensus on an appropriate level of antibiotic prescribing. But some experts said the new study's results are disturbing and that rates are probably excessive even in states with the lowest antibiotic prescription levels.

Antibiotics have been commonly available since the 1940s and have worked wonders saving patients with infections ranging from pneumonia to sexually spread diseases. But bacteria have increasingly gained the power to shrug off these drugs.

Experts say chances of resistance increase when antibiotics are not used long enough or are taken for the wrong reasons, allowing bacteria to survive and adapt. The Centers for Disease Control and Prevention is tracking at least 20 strains of resistant bacteria.

CDC researchers conducted the new study, analyzing a 2010 national database for prescription drugs. The findings were published in Thursday's New England Journal of Medicine.

Other studies have focused on antibiotic prescriptions for specific groups such as Medicare patients. This is the first to look at it for all Americans.

Doctors and other health care providers prescribed 258 million courses of antibiotics in 2010, for a population just shy of 309 million, the researchers found. That translates to 833 antibiotic prescriptions for every 1,000 people, on average.

But rates were much higher in West Virginia, Kentucky and Tennessee, where about 1,200 were written for every 1,000 people.

On the low end were Alaska, Oregon and California, where prescriptions were at or below 600.

Hawaii also was at the lower end of the scale with 646 prescriptions for every 1,000 people. Earlier studies found similar geographic trends.

Why the difference?

One possibility: Southerners suffer more infections than people in other parts of the country.

Southern states have the highest rates of obesity and diabetes, and diabetics tend to have more infections than other people, noted the CDC's Dr. Lauri Hicks, one of the study's authors.

"So some of that prescribing may be warranted," she said.

But the CDC study found the most frequently prescribed antibiotic was azithromycin, which is used for bronchitis symptoms. But bronchitis is usually caused by a virus, and antibiotics like azithromycin don't work against viruses.

***

ON THE NET:

>> *www.nejm.org*

Christmas Letter to Jeanine McCullagh

The following letter I wrote in response to a letter by Jeanine McCullagh. Jeanine is the wife of Bob McCullagh, who served as the Director of the Wesley Foundation. Wesley was a student center—my "home away from home" from 1958-1962. I include the letter, however, to show my early thoughts about reinventing health care, which I'll elaborate on more in the next chapter.

Dec. 15, 2010

Dear Jeanine:

Thank you for your very meaningful Christmas message. I appreciated very much the poem you sent.

I'm glad you are traveling to visit family members during the year…your grandchildren must be growing fast.

My son Bob is still single so I still don't have any grandchildren. He is the youth counselor for around thirty youth/young adults at the Waipahu Filipino United Church of Christ, so his life is very meaningful and purposeful. As long as he is happy doing what he was called to do with his special gifts, I am happy as a mother. I have thirty grandchildren so to speak. When I go to church, everyone refers to me as "Bob's Mom." His church work is as a volunteer, so he survives as a videographer.

As for myself, I continue to work with Micronesians here in Hawai'i. They are the newest immigrant group and have many issues, most related to not knowing the English language well.

I just added a new mission in life: to reinvent health care in the U.S.—away from a pharmaceutical-controlled system to a natural alternative health system using essential oils and other natural health gifts from God such as laughter, exercise, whole foods. I have not been to a doctor since Bob was born forty-one years ago and hope not to see one for the next forty years. My mom and dad never went and were healthy all their lives (which I interpret as meaning that pharmaceutical drugs and over-the-counter drugs are synthetic and toxic to the body in a cumulative sense). My mother always knew what to do as an Okinawan mother—making her own medicines from whole foods or plants. So I think this is my new mission in life.

I would appreciate your e-mail address; I will send photos of Bob and me and hope you can send photos of you and your children/grandchildren.

Blessings in this advent season and the new year ahead!

Love, Julia and Bob

Reinventing Health Care

About three years ago, I was introduced to the DoTerra mission of "Reinventing Health Care." Allyse and Patrick Sedivy spoke to a large group in Honolulu indicating that Americans spend $2.7 trillion on health care per year. And if you ask yourself and others whether we are healthier as a nation in the light of the $2.7 trillion spent, the usual answer is "No."

Our medical system is driven by profit. Health insurance companies, Big Pharma corporations, and private hospitals all promote disease management before employing strategies for prevention or cure that are best for the patients. I could write an entire book on real experiences with a dysfunctional health care system through the experiences of my husband, my mother, and many of my extended family members and friends.

Therefore, I immediately resonated with the call to "Reinvent Health Care" put out by the Sedivys in their many trips to Hawai'i. DoTerra means "gift of the earth," and the company, DoTerra International, gave me an opportunity to help my family and friends address the root causes of their health problems and not their symptoms.

I have set up two websitse as educational tools for all those who want to join the "Reinventing Health Care" movement. There are many videos on the site that show that the movement is gaining much steam. For example, one video shows how hospitals are joining the movement, and independent research results at medical schools and institutions are shared on the website as well. Please send me your feedback after viewing the videos and instructional materials and here's hoping you will join the "Reinventing Health Care" movement. The links are: www.keikomatsuihiga.com and www.thatdoterragal.com

I also have recently previewed a video on YouTube that illustrates the crying need to "Reinvent Health Care." Search for *"Escape Fire: The Fight To Rescue American Healthcare"* on Google, and this powerful film will move you to action.

Following is a little information from my website about my interest in Essential Oils as a preventative health care measure:

How Can Essential Oils Help You Live a Healthy Life?

Throughout history, essential oils have been used for not only medicinal, but therapeutic therapies. Egyptians, who were some of the first to use essential oils, used them for such things as:

- Beauty treatments
- Food preparation
- Religious ceremonies
- Medical treatments

What is an Essential Oil?

Essential oils are natural oils that are extracted from various parts of plants...bark, seeds, stems, roots, and flowers. These oils are not only fragrant, but they help the plant during pollination and also help provide protection.

Essential oils can be used aromatically, topically, and internally. They are very powerful and totally safe. Some of their uses are:

- Lemon oil can be used for cleansing and elevating your mood
- Peppermint oil can be used for indigestion
- Lemongrass can be used to calm cramping muscles
- Oil of Cloves can help relieve pain and can help draw toxins from your body
- Oil from Lavender is typically used to calm, reduce stress, and encourage sleep

I believe in the power, the effectiveness, and the safety of using essential oils. That is why I use only 100 percent pure Therapeutic Oils from doTERRA. I know they can benefit your health and wellness as they have benefited mine.

I primarily use them for their anti-aging properties.

Contact me to see how they can make a difference in your life.

Essential Oils Cough Syrup
www.facebook.com/EverydayEssentialOils

Add 3 drops OnGuard, 2 drops Lemon, and 1 drop of Eucalyptus to 1 teaspoon of honey on a spoon. Repeat every hour or two until pain subsides. Continue then 2 or 3 times a day for at least two days.

Comfort Food

A pidgin English poem based on a true event that happened while writing this book.

My computah wen go crash
Wen I needed the buggah the most
No can make deadline
Too much pilikia (trouble)
No can sleep
No can eat

Run to buy computah@Office Depot
Take home, still no work da buggah
Call da Hawaiian Tel tech guy
Voice recording sez everyting down fo one whole week
My heart go jugga jugga
Nuttin going right

Wasa matta I think
Maybe not nuf 'oinori'
Wen tings go bad
My pidgin com back
Cuz pidgin first talk talk kid time
Pidgin is da kine comfort food

I call Bob
Ur mom in trouble

Rush ovah o.k?
Bob rush ovah
We go to Hide-chan
Our fav mom and pop eatin place

Order Okinawan champuru and oyako don
Fo real dis is comfort food
Den everyting o.k.
Maddah and fadduh still looking ovah us
No mo pilikia
Tomorrow for shua everyting o.k.

The End

Champuru dish with bitter melon; Hide-chan Restaurant on corner of
South King and Hausten Streets.

Epilogue: Awareness and Action

I would like to end on a positive note, but throughout this book I have discussed some real issues that face our world, so I want to conclude with a call for awareness. We cannot change the world if we are not aware and realistic about the problems that face it. And so I wish to end by emphasizing Martin Luther King's statement on the three evils existing today that are at the root of human suffering: Racism, Militarism, and Extreme Materialism. Unfortunately, King also realized that today the United States is largely responsible for these evils, calling it, "the greatest purveyor of violence in the world, today."

Recently, I was made aware by the **Malu ʻAina Center** here in Hawaiʻi of an article by Glen Ford titled "America on MLK's Birthday: The Trifecta of Evils." Ford is a distinguished radio show host, who launched the first nationally syndicated Black news interview program on commercial television, the first nationally syndicated Hip Hop music show, co-founded the Black Commentator and launched the Black Agenda Report. He is also the author of *The Big Lie: An Analysis of U.S. Media Coverage of the Grenada Invasion*.

Below are excerpts from Ford's article discussing each of King's three evils and how they are still in operation in our world today. I encourage my readers to read full article online at: http://www.informationclearinghouse.info/article37454.htm

> **Racism:** "The U.S. prison population is by far the largest on the planet, in sheer numbers and in the proportion of Americans locked up. No other country comes close—which makes the United States the superpower of mass incarceration... Nearly half of U.S. prisoners are African American, although Blacks are only one-eighth of the total U.S. population." [By comparison, in Hawai'i, Dr. RaeDeen Keahiolalo-Karasuda, Ph.D. says that 3/5 of prisoners are Native Hawaiians while only 1/5 of the population.]

> **Militarism:** "The U.S. military budget is almost as large as the military spending of all the world's other nations, combined. Together, the U.S. and its NATO allies account for more than 70 percent of global weapons spending. At last count, the U.S. spent six times more on war than China, and 11 times more than Russia."

> **Extreme Materialism:** "By that, Dr. King meant great disparities in wealth and income. According to the *Suisse Global Wealth Databook*, wealth is so unevenly distributed in the United States, it no longer resembles a First World country. Of all the rich nations, the U.S. is dead last in terms of material equality."

In closing, I ask my readers: Now that you are aware of these evils, what action will you take to change them? If we each take up the responsibility of working against the evils in this world, then we can have a positive epilogue to our story.

To find out how to help take action to change the world, I encourage you to get involved with a group working for change. One such group here in Hawai'i is the Malu `Aina Center for Non-Violent Education & Action, which introduced me to the article by Glen Ford. Below is an excerpt from one of its flyers with contact information if you want to become involved. If you're not in Hawai'i, seek out another local or national organization and get involved.

Never Give Up! We Shall Overcome! Resist with Aloha!

1.Mourn all victims of violence.
2. Reject war as a solution.
3. Defend civil liberties.
4. Oppose all discrimination, anti-Islamic,
anti-Semitic, anti-Hawaiian, etc.
5. Seek peace through justice in Hawai'i
and around the world.

**Malu `Aina Center for Non-violent Education & Action
P.O. Box 489 Ola'a (Kurtistown), Hawai'i 96760.
Phone (808) 966-7622 Email ja@malu-aina.org
http://www.malu-aina.org**

A Final Note

Because of my love of books, it has always been my dream to produce a book of my own. With the encouragement of the Spirit of Children participants in Maine during this past summer and the Patrick Snow team, this book has become a reality.

What started out as a memoir ended up being a commentary about important passions in my life with a focus on "service" and "health" because of the influence of the Mokichi Okada Association (MOA) and the various spiritual groups that have formed a foundation for my life from 1940 to the present.

I hope the readers of this book will range from young adults to centenarians. I want to encourage people to give me feedback for the second edition I'm already working on. And I want to encourage all my readers to write their own books and share their stories with the wider community. It has become a spiritual and a healing journey for me and it will be so for anyone who enters the same stream and ocean. If you need encouragement and hints on how to become an author, do not hesitate to write to me at: tristar@hula.

net. "Talking story" means a two-way engagement; I look forward to continuing conversations with my readers.

Much aloha,

Julia Keiko Matsui
Higa Estrella

Appendices

'OHANA MEANS FAMILY

Poster Designed by Nancy Hom

Review Mirror[1]

by Bob Sigall

Wahiawa

I spoke to the Wahiawa Historical Society last month in a beautiful room at the Wahiawa Botanical Gardens. They inspired me to write a column of interesting facts about their city.

The name Wahiawa means a place of noise, loud or rumbling. It may come from surf on the north shore, nine miles away, that could he heard in ancient times.

King Kamehameha IV named the area Leilehua, and King Kalakaua built a hunting lodge there in the 1870s, where today's Schofield Barracks golf course clubhouse stands.

A group of mainlanders led by Byron Clark came to Wahiawa in 1898 because they were told it was the only piece of land on Oahu that was available for settlement. I believe California Avenue was so named because most of the settlers were from there. In two years, the population of the Wahiawa Colony Tract had grown to 80.

The settlers founded Wahiawa Elementary School in 1899. The first teacher of two boys and six girls was Adeline Clark.

James Dole came to Wahiawa in 1900. He bought 61 acres for $4,000. Locals scoffed at the 23-year old's dream of selling canned Wahiawa pineapple in every grocery store in America. Dole knew little about pineapples or canning but learned quickly.

Schofield Barracks was named for John Schofield, who was sent to see if Pearl Harbor would make a suitable navy base in 1872. He thought the entire U.S. and British navies could easily port there if the entrance was dredged.

A fort defends itself. A barracks houses troops that defend a different place, former Schofield Barracks commander General Fred Weyand told me. So, what was Schofield Barracks built to defend? Surprisingly, it was intended to defend Pearl Harbor from an overland attack from the north shore. I'll write more about Schofield Barracks in a future column.

Wahiawa General Hospital grew out of an emergency medical facility set up during World War II. It began at Wahiawa Elementary School. When the community's first hospital, Oahu Sugar Plantation Hospital closed in 1956, the community rallied to turn the civil defense clinic into a hospital, and Wahiawa General opened in 1957.

Many nisei townspeople joined the 442nd Infantry Battalion during World War II. The people of Wahiawa threw them a going away luau. When they arrived at Camp Selby, Mississippi, they found the town had collected and sent them $800 to use as they needed.

Plantation workers lived in over a dozen camps surrounding Wahiawa. In 1947, Hawaiian Pine consolidated several of its distant camps into Whitmore Village, a mile north of the city. John Whitmore was Dole's first Wahiawa plant manager, says Lani Nedbalek in the book *Wahiawa: From Dream to Community*.

Leilehua High School was originally on base and named Schofield High and Grammar School. It became a territorial high school in 1926—Oahu's second, after McKinley. Its mascot, the mule, is the same as the army's. After it settled into its new location after World War II, the *Honolulu Star-Bulletin* called it the "school of tomorrow."

Chez Michel's restaurant began in Wahiawa in 1942. Michel Martin had officers lining up for his French onion soup, duck l'orange, and frog legs. In 1959, he moved to the Colony Surf in Waikiki.

Kemoo Farm, outside Schofield Barracks, was founded as a pig and dairy farm in 1914 by Percy Pond. Within 20 years, the farm added a milk depot, ice cream parlor, coffee shop, and market. Kemoo means "lizard or reptile." Their best selling product was pineapple macadamia Happy Cakes.

Marian Harada opened Dot's restaurant in 1939 and named it for her sister. Its first name, in 1935, was the Sukiyaki Inn. Harada opened a skating rink in 1938 called the Wahiawa Amusement Center. Dot's Drive Inn took over their spot a year later and is still there today.

Servco opened as a two-car garage in Waialua in 1919. They moved to Wahiawa in the 1920s. Founder Peter Fukunaga held a contest to name the new company. The $25 prize was won by a Schofield sergeant who suggested Service Motor Company because service was the company's focus.

Schofield Barracks has so many interesting stories, that I'll save most of them for a future column.

1 I thought my readers would enjoy this article giving some of Wahiawa's history. This piece was first printed in the *Honolulu Star Advertiser* and is reprinted with permission. Bob Sigall is also the author of *The Companies We Keep*, a series of three books containing amazing stories about Hawaii's people, places, and companies. Sigall's books are available at most bookstores and www.CompaniesWeKeep.com

Best friends of Julia—Paztora Refalopei and children,
who moved to Hawai'i from Chu'uk State, Micronesia.

Julia, Roger, and Bob at Jeff Murakami's wedding in Honolulu,
June 1989. Jeff's sisters are Margaret, Joanne, and Joyce
(the children of these 3 are on page 38)

Tokyo Sky Tree (Ayako's father was one of the engineers to build this Sky Tree, the tallest building in Japan.)

Yguaran Family who adopted us on our Baha'i Pilgrimage.

Pidgin Test

PURPOSE: To explore the idea that so-called I.Q. tests usually measure experience, not intelligence.

DIRECTIONS

Indicate only one answer for each of the following questions.

1. "Kaka-roach" is another term for _____.
   a. rip-off
   b. nibble
   c. make out
   d. score
   e. hip

2. "Da makule guys" refers to _____.
   a. musicians
   b. hoodlums
   c. athletes
   d. senior citizens
   e. youths

3. A woman who is "hapai" is _____.
   a. available
   b. married
   c. pregnant
   d. sexy
   e. a mother

4. The opposite of "pilau" is _____.
   a. sad
   b. good
   c. cold
   d. sour
   e. ambitious

5. A "puka" is a _____.
   a. fish
   b. star
   c. curve
   d. hole
   e. vine

6. A "paniolo" is a _____.
   a. fisherman
   b. hunter
   c. policeman
   d. cowboy
   e. lover

7. "Da uddah time....."means ____
   a. milking time
   b. once before
   c. once upon a time
   d. What's the time?
   e. sometime in the future

8. "Jag-up" refers to a person who is
   a. in jail
   b. broke
   c. in trouble
   d. drunk
   e. in love

9. A "niele" person is one who is ___
   a. quiet
   b. lazy
   c. curious
   d. generous
   e. sly

10. "Huli 'um" means to _____.
    a. share it
    b. turn it over
    c. tuck it up
    d. lift it up
    e. throw it out

(GO ON)

11. Which word is most out of place here?
    a. haupia
    b. poi
    c. kalua pig
    d. loko
    e. hanai

12. "Hemo", as in "Hemo your jacket",
    means to _____.
    a. put on
    b. bring
    c. zip
    d. hang
    e. remove

13. "Huki the rope" means to _____.
    a. cut the rope into pieces
    b. splice the rope
    c. hold on to the rope
    d. tie the rope
    e. pull the rope

14. "You get stink ear" means that you _____.
    a. only listen to negative things
    b. have wax in ;your ear
    c. don't listen well
    d. try to hear all the gossip you can
    e. are capable of hearing the voices of
       spirits

15. A Hana store made famous by a song is
    _____.
    a. Tamashiro's General Store
    b. Arakawa's General Store
    c. Hasegawa's General Store
    d. Hana's Dairy Bar
    e. Safeway

16. If you were a "luna" one of your jc
    would be to _____.
    a. arrest
    b. supervise
    c. preach
    d. milk
    e. shop

17. A person ;who does something
    irritating or annoying may be
    described as being _____.
    a. mahaoe
    b. tutu
    c. akahi
    d. akule
    e. nahino

18. If a person is called "swell-head",
    then he is probably _____.
    a. nursing a hangover
    b. angry
    c. conceited
    d. a show-off
    e. a politician

19. If you live on the "mauka" side of
    street, then your home is probabl
    _____.
    a. on the east side
    b. on the west side
    c. on the south side
    d. toward the mountains
    e. toward the ocean

20. If someone gives you something
    "manuwahi", it means that_____.
    a. it's free
    b. you should return a gift of equa
       value
    c. you should return a gift of highe
       value
    d. you should pay its monetary va
    e. you should never accept it aftei
       sunset

(GO ON)

21. If someone from the crowd yells "Hana hou!" to an entertainer, he's telling the entertainer _____.
   a. get off the stage
   b. to do another number
   c. to sing louder
   d. that he's "far out"
   e. that he's lousy

22. If you drive from Hana to Kahului (52 miles), the common understanding among people is that it will take you _____.
   a. 2 hours
   b. 3 hours
   c. 4 hours
   d. 1 1/2 hours
   e. 45 minutes

23. "Pau hana time come by my house" means _____.
   a. When you have a chance, come to my house.
   b. After dinner, come over to my house.
   c. Come over to my house this evening.
   d. Come over to my house after work.
   e. Come over to my house in the morning.

24. If a student told his teacher, "Teacha, Kaina kukai him pants", it means that Kaina _____.
   a. messed his pants
   b. ripped his pants
   c. wet his pants
   d. burnt his pants
   e. took off his pants

25. If someone ;would say that dinner was delicious, he probably would say that it was _____.
   a. papa's
   b. kukui
   c. ewa
   d. lolo
   e. ono

26. "Pakalolo" is _____.
   a. salted raw fish and seaweed
   b. whiskey made from the ti root
   c. marijuana
   d. liquor
   e. acid

27. A person with a "pakiki head" is one who is _____.
   a. shrewd
   b. business-minded
   c. bald
   d. stubborn
   e. an egghead

28. "Hana-butta" is known statewide as _____.
   a. high-fat butter made in Hana
   b. margarine from the Hana Dairy
   c. a famous peanut butter shake from Tutu's Snack Bar, Hana
   d. mucous running from the nose person with a bad cold
   e. a peanut butter sandwich

29. If you were at home and someon told you to get them "da kine", the would probably mean _____.
   a. a glass of water
   b. a towel
   c. an ash tray
   d. dried fish
   e. any of the above

30. "Jun-ken a mun-ken a sucka sucl po; Wailuku, Wailuku bum bum show." This is _____.
   a. a jingle kids use in playing follc the leader
   b. a pidgin drinking song
   c. a jingle used in playing "duck-c goose"
   d. a pidgin nursery rhyme
   e. a phrase used in selecting whc goes first in a game

Test Created by Hawai'i State House Representative Roy Takumi

FOR ANSWERS GO TO: www.keikomatsuihiga.com

About the Author

Julia Keiko Matsui Higa Estrella was born in Wahiawa, Oahu, Hawai'i on December 26, 1940. She wrote *Being Local in Hawai'i* as both a memoir and commentary on the passions in her life: Service and Health. She graduated from Wahiawa Elementary, Leilehua Intermediate and High School, University of Hawai'i at Manoa, Claremont School of Theology and University of California at Berkeley. In addition to Hawaii, she has lived in Claremont, Oakland, Sacramento, and Berkeley, California. She also served as a city planner for the City of Las Vegas.

She credits the important foundation of her life as being the unconditional love she received from her parents Kyozo and Matsuo Higa Matsui, her sister Ruth Matsui Murakami, her husband Rogelio Estrella, and her son Robert Estrella.

Julia wants her readers to be inspired by her stories and become actively involved in important issues of the day. Furthermore, she believes the best gift one can give one's children, grandchildren, and great-grandchildren is to be healthy and fit (with mind and body intact) as a centenarian.

A video interview of Julia, telling her story and how she became a local and political activist, can be viewed as part of the Journey to Justice series produced by Hegemony Studies. In this interview, Julia discusses her three arrests: protesting against the University of California, Berkeley's policy to invest in apartheid South Africa (1974), protesting the U.S. military testing of missiles (Star Wars) on sacred Hawaiian lands on Kauai (1993), and demonstrating against the City of Honolulu's decision to close Ala Moana Park to the homeless (2006). Estrella considers "arrests" to be an important political tool to bring public awareness to social justice issues. The video can be viewed at www.hegemonystudies.org or http://vimeo.com/42015648

Visit Julia online and continue to "talk story" with her at:

www.KeikoMatsuiHiga.com
and
www.ThatDoTerraGal.com